Stables and other Equestrian Buildings

Stables and other Equestrian Buildings

A Guide to Design and Construction

KEITH WARTH

dipl. Arch RIBA

J. A. Allen
LONDON

Photograph opposite title page: *New stables in a greenfield setting. Considerable tree planting will soon give the site a mature appearance.*

British Library Cataloguing-in-Publication Data.
A Catalogue record for this book is available from the British Library.

ISBN 0.85131.687.5

Published in Great Britain in 1997 by
J. A. Allen & Company Limited,
1 Lower Grosvenor Place, Buckingham Palace Road,
London, SW1W OEL

Typeset and designed by Judy Linard
Illustrations by Keith Warth
Photographs by Shutterbug Photography
Colour processing by Tenon & Polert Colour Scanning Ltd., Hong Kong
Printed by Dah Hua Printing Press Co. Ltd., Hong Kong

Contents

Contents

Preface

I lay no claim to being an expert on horses but my experience as an architect, involved in the design of equestrian buildings over many years, has led me to the conclusion that a horse's innate ability cannot be improved by its surroundings. However, it is possible to improve its well-being and performance by designing an environment to enable a horse to achieve its full potential and to eliminate conditions which could have a detrimental effect.

This statement holds good for all horses, from the fleetest Thoroughbred racehorse, the most competitive eventer and most valuable brood mare right down to my daughter's sturdy little Welsh Mountain pony. It also holds good for equine establishments costing vast amounts of money through to those comprising modest stables. The principles of good design are exactly the same. It costs no more to build or renovate a stable to a good design than to a poor design, but the benefits of good design can be enormous.

This work is intended to assist anyone contemplating improving or constructing equine accommodation and related buildings. Although addressed to the serious equine establishment, as mentioned above the principles hold equally good for more modest ventures including those with a pony 'at the bottom of the garden' so I have included a small section for the keen amateur.

The book looks at the various elements involved in stable design and provides information on the main requirements for the horse and the efficient workings of an equine establishment. It also looks at the basic accommodation requirements and legislation which may have to be taken into account in any new building or refurbishment project. In addition, it provides a comprehensive guide to construction, materials and services that are a necessity in any stable yard.

I very much doubt that anyone will agree with every thing I have suggested - there are as many opinions on the correct way to look after horses as there are on bringing up children - all strongly held and vociferously defended. However, the aim is to put forward my ideas and suggestions to provoke thought and consideration in the design of equine buildings, hopefully resulting in a better environment for the horse.

Some of our predecessors early in the twentieth century

used their great knowledge of horses to provide stables with equally good conditions for the horse as would be recommended today, particularly in respect of ventilation. It is therefore astonishing that, despite the knowledge gained from recent research, stables are still being built which fail to provide good conditions for the horse due to lack of design consideration.

As an architect, the impact of the built environment and the sensitive nature of new buildings in a rural setting is of concern to me; protection of the countryside must be an important consideration in any new design. This does not mean there should be no rural development. On the contrary, diversification from existing traditional farming to equine-related establishments is a valuable way of protecting the countryside by assisting the rural economy.

The main aim of owning a horse is for it to be available to do its work, at whatever level, when required. After long hours of hard work preparing for an outing, for the horse to be 'unavailable' through illness or injury is extremely frustrating. If the 'unavailability' means missing a race or event it could have significant commercial implications; if it means missing a long-anticipated gymkhana it is equally disappointing for the rider. The intention of good stable design is to eliminate any possibility of the built environment inadvertently contributing towards that 'unavailability'. Moreover, with knowledge from recent research and careful planning, the design should actively deter some potential equine problems to the benefit of the animal's physical and mental well-being and the increased enjoyment by the owner.

There has been a significant increase in the popularity of the horse in recent years, particularly in the leisure sector and the horse population in the UK is greater today than at any time in our history. Investment in well designed, aesthetically pleasing equestrian building should therefore prove to be an asset to any property.

Acknowledgements

I could not have completed a book with such varied content without the help of many people. I am grateful to Charlie Oakshott and Michael Russell for their assistance and Dr David Coates for his support. I am mostly indebted to my wife Lynda for her patience and help over many months and for encouraging me to complete the work.

Photographs

I would particularly like to thank Brian D. Hatson, Shutterbug Photography, for his time and effort in producing the high quality photographs in this book.

Introduction

The working horse is an athlete and its physical condition is paramount to its performance. In particular, the competition horse needs excellent heart and lungs and sound legs. Both the respiratory system and the horses' legs can be directly affected by stable design.

Just as the physical condition of a horse can be impaired by poor environmental conditions in the stable, the horse's health and performance can be improved by good conditions. It is therefore essential that the basic enclosure of the stable provides conditions that allow the animal to flourish.

Basic stable requirements

The principal requirements dictating the design and construction of a stable box, whether it be for a competition horse, commercial horse or fun pony are:

- dryness
- warmth
- fresh air (draught free)

- hygiene and safety
- natural light.

In addition to the horse's needs are the requirements of the stable staff; these can be summarised as follows:

- safe and easy access to boxes
- visual supervision and security of the animal
- proximity of water, feed and bedding material to the boxes
- ease of removal of waste matter
- artificial light.

The ultimate value of good stable design should not be underestimated. Apart from their failure to function well, poorly built and ill-considered stable boxes do not last very long. Deterioration of the building fabric can leave cracks, crevices, ponding and other defects which can have a negative effect on the well-being of the horse and its performance. Similarly, poorly maintained buildings encourage vermin and are detrimental to the image of a well-run enterprise.

1

Opposite: *Attractive traditional stables in a mature setting.*

In more detail the principal requirements are:

DRYNESS

The stable should be watertight with no rain penetration through the roof, walls or windows. To protect the stable still further, a larger roof overhang is frequently provided over the stable door to restrict ingress of driving rain. As a generally rule it is good practice to provide a reasonable size roof overhang all round the building to protect the walls and windows from rain.

Internally, the floor should be laid to a fall to remove any water/urine from within the box as dampness, even in the bedding, will eventually evaporate and lead to a damp atmosphere.

WARMTH

Warmth is provided by the building enclosure protecting the animal from the elements. In general, no heating is required within a stable unless it is for a special use such as foaling or a sick animal. The 'comfort' heat that exists in an average box is only the result of body heat given off by the animal. To retain some of this warmth the ceiling can be insulated which not only reduces the heat loss but creates a warm ceiling surface that greatly reduces the risk of condensation.

Should occasional heating be required in a stable for an injured or sick animal then this is usually best provided by infra-red lamps; infra-red being particularly suitable for replacing lost body heat from the animal without heating the surrounding air.

FRESH AIR

Fresh air should be continually available and stale air should be expelled. This does not usually require mechanical extraction as good ventilation can be achieved by careful provision and positioning of adequate air inlets and vents when the building is being designed. Fresh air

and ventilation are two of the foremost pre-requisites in the environmental conditions of the stabled horse and today it is considered by many that increased rates of draught-free ventilation can actually reduce the risk of infection.

HYGIENE AND SAFETY

The stable should be constructed of materials that are easy to clean, moisture resistant and able to withstand regular washing or steam cleaning. The floor, particularly, should be free of hollows that may retain urine and encourage infection. The stable interior should also have no protrusions on which the animal could injure itself and arrises, such as at door openings, should either be rounded off or protected by rollers.

LIGHT

Daylight is essential for the horse's well-being. Sunlight, in particular, is necessary for the growth of an animal and even has an effect on hormonal balance. Artificial light is essential in any stable, not only to carry out regular management tasks and to check the well-being of the animal after dark, but it is also essential for emergencies during the hours of darkness.

Standard of stable provision

The constructional requirement of a stable varies depending on the type of animal and what the animal is used for. At the most basic level, the family pony may require little more from the stable than four walls and a roof, especially if it is a native breed. Indeed, the horse may well be out in the paddock in all but the very worst weather and for this reason it would not make sense to provide an overelaborate building.

If the animal is more highly bred, is constantly in work

2

Opposite: *Sympathetic conversion of a barn to form stables.*

or is clipped, this will dictate that the building should afford a greater degree of protection from the weather. Consequently, the standard of stable provision will need to be higher. This degree of protection may also be affected by the value of the horse as security is likely to be of some importance.

Even the same breed of horse serving a different purpose may need greatly differing stable standards; a Thoroughbred broodmare and a Thoroughbred racehorse in training are good examples. A Thoroughbred racehorse in training spends almost all its time in the stable and will require a space that provides freedom and interest to occupy it actively and comfortable conditions to help it to recover from stressful exertions. Conversely, a Thoroughbred brood mare which is in a paddock for most of the day will require a larger but less elaborate box in terms of windows, interest and resilient floor.

The use to which the horse is put is therefore relevant to the standard of provision for that particular stable. However, all horses will need the fundamentals of hygienic and safe conditions.

The previous paragraphs discuss the provision of stable accommodation from the physical point of view. However, in its natural environment the horse is a herd animal. If the stable design takes account of the way the animal behaves in nature then the horse is less likely to be bored or agitated and to indulge in unwanted behaviour. The horse's mental as well as physical well-being is therefore a consideration and attention to this aspect in the building design is more likely to result in a contented horse. A contented horse, in turn, is less likely to use up nervous energy and more likely to perform to its full potential.

Peter Gray MRCVS, in his book *Respiratory Diseases*, gives some excellent information on the theories why modern horses appear more prone to illness and pneumonia. He refers to veterinary books written in 1868 and 1869 by W. J. Miles and Lieutenant General Fitzwygram, which postulate that a more equitable temperature in the stable of about 50-60 °F (10-15 °C) is necessary for the horse's well-being. Peter Gray suggests that stable temperatures in this range may be of great benefit in the treatment of many respiratory illnesses and may also help to reduce the risk of respiratory illness.

The increased incidence of respiratory infection over the past few years has also been linked to the use of American barn stables. In addition, veterinary research has shown that there is a link between respiratory infection and the degree of fungal spores in hay and straw bedding.

Recent research and modern theory have placed greater importance on the horse's welfare being improved by significantly higher levels of draught-free ventilation than previously were thought necessary and which exist in the majority of older stables. Stable design should take account of the knowledge gained over the years by veterinary researchers, particularly the importance of excellent ventilation. If this knowledge is applied to the design of new stable buildings then the horses' well-being and performance can be expected to improve.

It is not essential to 'purpose build' all stable buildings. Quite effective stables can be created from old buildings and many good stables have been converted from, for example, former dairy buildings. Indeed, the conversion of an old barn provides an ideal enclosure, with the considerable height giving an abundance of fresh air, so vital as a basic necessity of a good stable.

Whenever a new development is proposed or an existing yard refurbished, the opportunity arises to create better conditions for the animals, increase the value of the property and, often, improve the image of the establishment.

Chapter One

New stable complexes

Briefing

It is exciting when any new development takes place. Once the decision to build has been made, there is a natural inclination to press ahead and to do so at break-neck speed. It should be remembered that the building is likely to be there for 50-100 years and time spent at the design stage to achieve the optimum development is insignificant compared with the overall life of the building. Additionally, it is much easier to alter lines on a drawing than to demolish and rebuild walls or, indeed, a whole building, therefore it is in everyone's interest to make sure the design and siting are totally satisfactory before the project starts on site.

A good design, well worked out and detailed, can often save money and time by avoiding unnecessary and expensive changes on site. Good briefing is the pre-requisite to good design and a satisfactory solution.

Equally detailed thought should be given to the overall layout of a small yard as to a large development on an estate. Future extensions or other possibilities should be considered in terms of a master plan, even if development of the master plan is very much in the long term. Certainly, with the increased sensitivity of building in the rural environment and the greater difficulties that can be thrown up by planning authorities, it is becoming essential that individual buildings are looked at and judged in the context of future plans for the establishment.

BEHAVIOURAL ASPECTS

As mentioned in the previous chapter, the horse is a natural herd animal and can benefit greatly if this natural instinct is taken into account in stable design. A very experienced stud manager convinced me some years ago of the importance of enabling this instinct to prevail. Among his many reasoned arguments were references to the need for brood mares to be able to see and 'communicate' with each other. He was of the opinion that if the buildings permitted the herd instinct to pervade, the brood mares became more contented. He firmly believed that this was a major factor which enabled his mares to achieve an exceptionally high percentage conception rate year after year.

In some stables this natural herd instinct is ack-

The sliding hatch gives flexibility to isolate the boxes when required.

nowledged and adjacent boxes, particularly for fillies, have vision grilles to enable the animals to communicate closely with each other. This is widely believed to reduce stress and boredom in the animals. The promotion of the herd instinct is not quite so easily achieved with colts due to their more aggressive nature but works well with geldings.

If behavioural problems are recognised in the design, and measures taken to provide an interest for the stabled horse, this is likely to reduce such things as box walking and other vices that use up nervous energy. In turn, the horse is more likely to apply its energy to the areas that will help its competitive performance.

Given the opportunity, the horse will often look out over its stable door to take an interest in what is happening in the world outside. An anti-weave grille attached to the bottom door allows the horse to put its head out but stops the vice of weaving.

For the permanently stabled horse an additional top door only in the back of the box (as well as a window) can be of enormous benefit to the horse. During periods when this door is open, the animal has double the potential activity to observe and be part of yard activity

and this will stimulate its mental well-being. In addition, the open top door at the rear of the stable increases the cross-flow ventilation, keeping the stable fresh. This additional top door in the rear of the box can be installed in all types of stables, whether traditional yards or American barns.

PHYSICAL ASPECTS

The competition horse needs a good heart, strong lungs and sound legs. The latter two can be assisted by good stable design. Two constructional areas that greatly affect these points are box ventilation and flooring.

The boxes must have thorough and effective ventilation. The horse's anatomy, with its respiratory passages close to its mouth, means that there is a risk of contagious spore infection from anything that it smells or eats. Much research has been carried out on fungal spores in hay and straw bedding and the pathogens within them. Infection in the respiratory tract or organs will seriously impede the horse's breathing ability and therefore its performance. It is recognised that good, continuous ventilation in the right place in a stable can dilute any contaminated air and help to expel it.

Regarding flooring, although not based on any proven scientific research, it is possible to assume that a horse standing on a very hard surface all day will be prone to aching and tired legs in just the same way that a human is affected by standing on hard floor finishes. It would seem logical that an animal which, in its natural state, stands on the softer surface of grassland would be far more comfortable with a resilient floor in its box. A resilient floor finish for a stable becomes more important for the animal that spends the majority of the time in its box than for the animal that is mostly in the paddock.

Concrete or brick flooring, surprisingly, seems to be the accepted norm in floor construction, with the resilience being provided by the bedding material.

If straw is used as the bedding, it is often left as a comparatively thick bed and a concrete floor may well be the best floor base. However, with the increasing use of shavings and shredded paper, which are far less resilient than straw, a more resilient floor base than concrete should be used.

Decisions on which type of bedding is to be used need to be established at the briefing stage as they will have an impact on the type of floor construction to be specified and also on other parts of the development, such as the size of the manure bunker.

Stable types

In terms of stable accommodation there are two basic forms: the traditional yard or the American barn. These are two completely different structure forms. In recent years, there has been a growing tendency in the UK to build boxes in an American barn format. This has primarily been to enable the owner to build in a more economical form and with greater advantages in the way of sophisticated and efficient services to the benefit of stable staff and the horses. A brief synopsis sets out the differences and some of the advantages and disadvantages of each of the two forms of building.

YARD

A traditional stable yard or open yard is composed of a group of individual boxes built side by side, often into a U-shape or sometimes into a complete courtyard arrangement.

It is usual for the yard also to contain ancillary accommodation such as tack room, feed room, hay/straw store, utility box and perhaps a mess room. On a stud farm the yard is, in addition, likely to contain a vet's

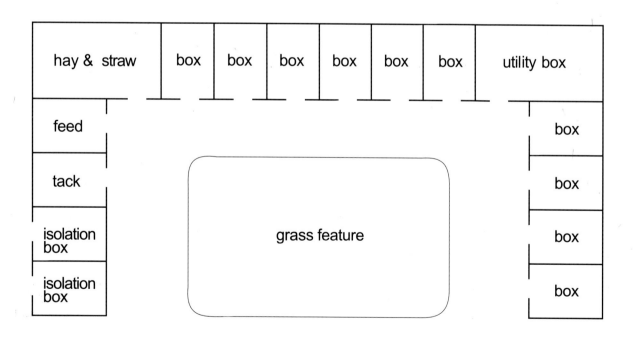

Basic layout of a traditional yard.

room and possibly a foaling unit.

Traditional yards are often considered to be aesthetically more attractive and where appearance is an important criteria, the traditional yard can be developed to form an interesting focal point. It is common practice for the roof to be topped with a cupola or a clock tower to add to the interest and sense of importance.

For a small number of boxes, the traditional yard format offers the most economical solution, with the option that the yard can easily be extended in the future.

On a site that is considered environmentally sensitive, the smaller, more domestic scale of traditional boxes is often favoured.

BARNS

The barn style of stabling or American barn is essentially a large span building containing many stable boxes under one roof, the individual stables being formed within the barn by prefabricated stable divisions or partition walls.

The British version of the American barn often has a central tractor-way with boxes on either side. Each box then has a door out on to the tractor-way, but usually only a window on the outside wall. The tractor-way must be wide enough for a tractor and trailer on to which the

manure from each box is loaded. This is a particularly economical form of construction when several stable boxes are required, due to its lower wall-to-roof ratio.

It is usual for the loose boxes to be divided from each other by only a part height wall. This means that the air within the whole barn is shared, with the inherently higher risk of cross infections due to the shared environmental conditions. The problem can be exacerbated if the roof pitch is low or, worse still, single-skin roofing is specified, leading to condensation and poor air quality. The large, open nature of the internal space does, however, allow the horses to communicate with each other and so promotes the herd instinct. The American barn format is also advantageous in that lighting, security and other services can be readily installed and can cover many stables *en masse*, making their provision much cheaper.

The advantage of an American barn for the stable hand is that all work is carried out under cover.

Although the barn arrangement originates from America, it is interesting to note that the design of some English Victorian yards, such as at Stanley House, Newmarket, although basically a traditional yard, are really a clever variation of the American barn arrangement. The

Typical layout of American barn.

Opposite: *Typical traditional yard.*
Next two pages: *Typical American barn.*
  Tractor-way with boxes on either side; note the high roof and insulated, easy to clean ceiling.

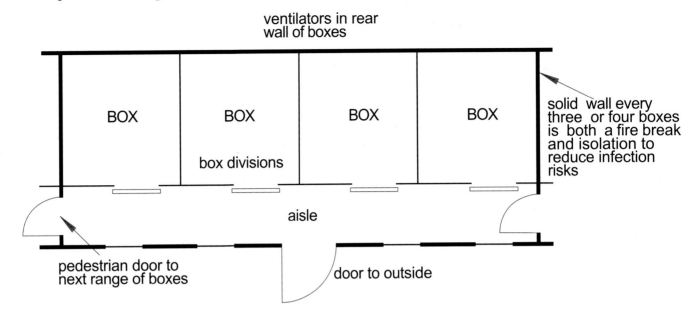

ventilators in rear
wall of boxes

BOX | BOX | BOX | BOX

box divisions

solid wall every
three or four boxes
is both a fire break
and isolation to
reduce infection
risks

aisle

pedestrian door to
next range of boxes

door to outside

Layout of inner aisle boxes.

boxes in the old yard at Stanley House stables are in groups of between two to four, with each group opening on to an internal walkway (aisle), which itself then opens on to the main courtyard.

This arrangement enables the animals to see and communicate with each other over the box divisions, which, in turn, helps to reduce boredom, fretting and wasted energy, but it also restricts the number of horses in close proximity to each other and so reduces the risk of cross-infection. The barrier created by the second door to the outside also reduces direct draughts on to the animals while allowing the stable lad/lass to carry out their work indoors.

Many French yards in Normandy are also constructed on the inner aisle principle but tend to have much wider internal accessways.

Whichever basic building format is adopted, all aspects of the design need to be agreed beforehand. On some projects, the briefing may extend into several sessions and include visits to existing establishments in order to understand the working practices that are to be adopted for the project in hand. After the full list of accommodation and briefing session(s) have been completed the initial sketches can be produced.

Design of a traditional yard

The yard should be orientated so that the majority of boxes have the benefit of the sun and, for this reason, it is usual for a southerly aspect to be selected. This orientation also shields the yard from the cold, winter north-easterly winds. If the yard faces south, then a roof overhang should be included above the front apron to prevent excessive direct sun's rays from shining into the boxes. The width of roof overhang will, to some extent, be dictated by the type of horses to be accommodated.

For an animal that is out in its paddock for most of the day, it may be advantageous to provide a roof overhang above the apron of approximately 1.5 m (5 ft) width to

Opposite: *Traditional stables with roof overhang.*

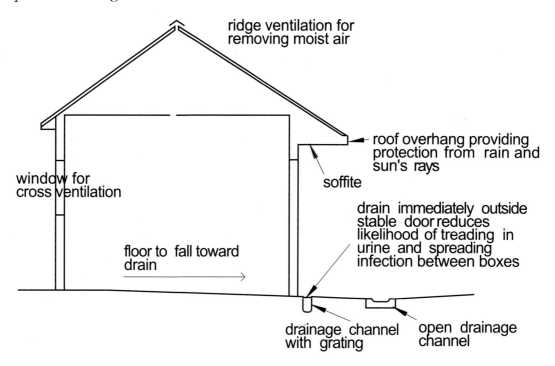

ridge ventilation for removing moist air

roof overhang providing protection from rain and sun's rays

window for cross ventilation

soffite

drain immediately outside stable door reduces likelihood of treading in urine and spreading infection between boxes

floor to fall toward drain

drainage channel with grating

open drainage channel

Typical elements of a box.

allow the stable hand to work under sheltered conditions.

The horse kept in its box for most of the day will have little chance to benefit from the sun's rays and therefore a reduced overhang of only 750 mm (30 in) is preferable in order simply to keep driving rain out of the box. This small overhang will still offer some protection to the stable hand while cleaning out the yard.

With the traditional yard format there is a wonderful opportunity to design excellent cross flow ventilation in the boxes and at the same time prohibit air transference between boxes, which greatly reduces the risk of spread of airborne infection between horses.

Where isolation of the animals is required and separation of air spaces becomes necessary, the traditional yard has a great physical advantage over the American barn format.

Whichever system of stabling is decided upon, it is worthwhile to design each box with fully openable

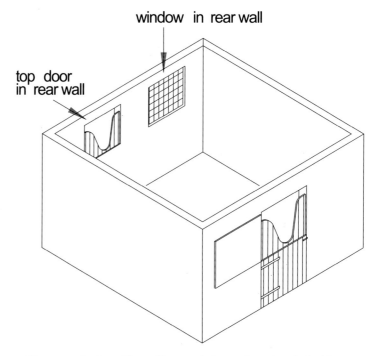

window in rear wall

top door in rear wall

Diagrammatic view of box with rear window and top door for looking out.

14

windows or doors at both the back and front, giving the box two aspects. This gives the animal two views of activities taking place outside and, in giving it some interest, reduces the chance of boredom and associated unwanted behaviour. Also, in good weather the horse can benefit from direct sunlight whatever the orientation of the building.

Boredom is less of a problem where the animals are in the paddock for most of the day. The main factors influencing design of the stable box then become hygiene, safety, security and supervision.

By its very form, when about 16 or fewer boxes are being built, the traditional yard is more economical to construct than an American barn as there is no need for a main structural frame.

Beyond 20 boxes, the American barn format is progressively more economical when compared with the open yard and should be considered if cost is the prime consideration.

Design of a barn

The regional climatic conditions will, to a large extent, be reflected in the type of building needed. In the North American state of Kentucky where there are often very cold winters, there has been a long history of building in a barn arrangement. This concept originated in Tennessee where an old tobacco barn was converted to stable several horses under one roof. This form of stabling proved very popular and it is now the most widespread form of stabling in America.

In its original form the converted tobacco barn provided a sound basis for conversion to stabling for horses. Invariably, the tobacco barns were constructed at the top of a hill where the wind provided ideal conditions for drying the tobacco and, in its new use, provided good ventilation for the stables.

The American barn style consists of several stable boxes on either side of an access passageway all under one roof. Although there are many variations in detail, the barns usually have boxes with a door on to the passageway and, in America, they often have another door from the box to the outside paddocks.

A distinct advantage of the American barn style of building is the opportunity it gives to provide sophisticated services and management to the benefit of stable hand and horse. Its use is therefore more applicable to the commercial or larger establishment.

On a stud farm, the American barn arrangement is particularly appropriate for housing barren mares. The barn format lends itself to the installation of special light fittings giving off light waves closely resembling those of natural daylight. These fittings have been proved to be very effective when connected to a time clock to mimic a longer day, thereby bringing the mare into season earlier in the year. On a commercial stud farm where the 'forwardness' of a foal has a great impact on the bids received at the sales, the cost of such lighting can be paid for in just one extra bid.

With the growing tendency for more two-year-old racing, together with more two-year-old racing at an early stage of the season, there is pressure on trainers by owners to get their animal racing early. Moderate to late foals can be as much as 20 per cent younger than a competitor in a two-year-old race. Even for the three-year-old classics early in the season, it is possible for a late foal to be 10-15 per cent less mature than a rival competitor, hence the ability to encourage early-season conception of a foal by light induction can be seen to be commercially beneficial. (See section on lighting, page 48.)

Another advantage of the barn system of building is that it lends itself readily to the use of modern building materials and technology. This is particularly apparent in

the products available for roof construction. Profiled aluminium roof sheeting is one such product which is available complete with insulating sandwich layer and underlining sheet. The sheets provide a self-finished, impervious, rot-proof roof which can be steam cleaned indefinitely and have a good light reflection value, giving a bright, airy appearance to the interior of the building. The sheets are large and can cover areas quickly and cheaply. Translucent sheets are available where daylight is required but these should always be specified as double glazed (skinned) to reduce problems with condensation.

The insulation in a 'sandwich' construction has many benefits not only for retaining some warmth in the barn, but also in reducing noise levels on the roof which, with some sheet materials, can be rather disturbing to the animals during heavy rain or hailstorms. The insulated sandwich construction also dramatically reduces the risk of condensation and dampness within the building which can be damaging to both the building and to the horses' health.

The large air volume of a barn promotes steady air movement while the cumulative heat given off from the animals helps to maintain an equilibrium of temperature.

It is common for the American barn type of building to include ancillary accommodation such as hay and straw stores, feed stores, tack room and maybe a turning out/exercise ring.

Another added benefit of the American barn style of building is in the other facilities that can be included within the building at a relatively modest cost. For

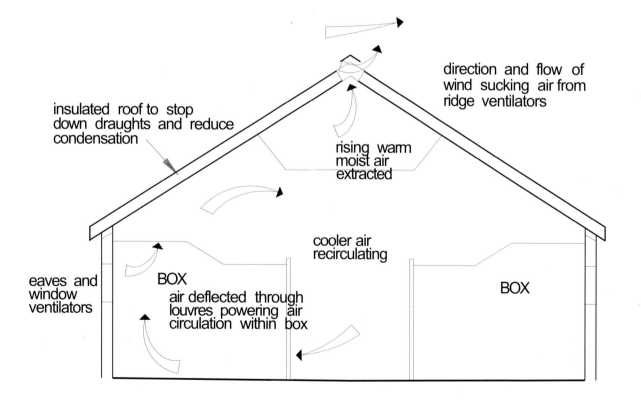

insulated roof to stop down draughts and reduce condensation

direction and flow of wind sucking air from ridge ventilators

rising warm moist air extracted

cooler air recirculating

eaves and window ventilators

BOX

air deflected through louvres powering air circulation within box

BOX

American barn air movements.

17

example, simple security and fire precaution systems can cover the entire building, protecting many horses. The same applies to the electronic insect killers widely used in American barns to rid the building of flies which irritate the horse. A single unit can cover an area of up to 139 sq m (1500 sq ft) which means that one unit can cover several boxes.

As the nature of a barn is a large-span structure, the central areas can be dark. For barns with corrugated sheet roofing, mention has been made of the use of translucent panels. For traditional roofing materials, such as slates and tiles, alternative provision needs to be made. To increase the natural light level in tiled or slated roofs there is the opportunity to design the roof with large glazed areas. These can either be the openable Velux type rooflights or fixed patent glazed panels. All should be located near the ridge where good, even light can be obtained without the problem of direct sun rays on to the animal in its box.

It is important that all glass in a stable complex should be laminated safety glass. As with all standard glass this cuts out the ultra-violet spectrum of the sun's rays, which helps to kill bacteria and stimulates the production of vitamin D within the animal. Special glass which allows ultra-violet rays through can be obtained but is considerably more expensive.

Chapter Two

Siting the stables

Once built, the building will be there for a very long time so very careful selection of the site is one of the most important decisions. The building itself can be modified or altered after it has been erected but the siting is going to remain the same for the duration.

Siting is therefore crucial and will be affected by numerous factors. These include aspect, prevailing winds, existing buildings, long-term intentions and the natural features of the site such as trees, shelter belts and paddocks. This is where an overall master plan can be of immense use. Each building, and its relationship with other buildings, is relevant and good planning should lead to a well-functioning establishment.

For small complexes the location of the stables is usually dictated by the proximity of existing buildings and the services available. On a stud farm, however, with the open countryside nature of the development, the choice of position is more flexible. For it to operate effectively, it is essential that the function of the buildings and estate are understood and taken into account in the initial planning.

Stable blocks on a stud farm are usually situated in isolation, surrounded by paddocks. The stables become no more than a night-time shelter as the mares and foals are turned out in a paddock during the day.

Stable buildings should never be placed at the lowest point of the site where there is a greater likelihood of frost pockets. The criteria regarding low-lying positions are quite important as various fundamental difficulties can arise from siting a building in a low spot. Firstly, there is the need to take storm water, surface water and foul waste away from the building and for this to be cost-effective the drains should discharge by gravity to fall away from the building. In addition, smaller nursery paddocks are generally located close to the boxes and if at a low point, the paddocks are more likely to become wet and boggy, leading to such ailments as foot rot. There is also a higher risk of injury to animals slipping into fencing while running at high speed.

Equally, the stables should not be on the highest or most exposed part of a site and should not be immediately adjacent to large trees or topography that may affect the free flow of air over and through the building. (See section on ventilation, page 43.)

Siting of buildings needs to be considered in relation to

the type of animal to be housed. A brood mare stable should not be near a weanling paddock or stables. Also yearlings, mares in foal and barren mares need to be kept away from each other as groups. These issues, together with the location of summer and winter paddocks, are essentially a management issue for the owner but need to be discussed as part of the briefing process.

The orientation of the stable boxes should achieve sunlight into each box. Frequently, however, the position of the building is dictated by other buildings on the site. An important factor in the siting of a stable is the efficiency of working within the yard which is, of course,

an invaluable cost saving for the owner.

Consideration also needs to be given to the siting of any staff accommodation. Visual security near the yard is desirable and if the development is a stud farm, the groom's accommodation needs to be located in close proximity to the foaling unit.

Additional staff accommodation may well be required on a larger equestrian establishment and this could be the main source of problems with the planning authority. Judicial siting and a well-argued case may need to be made to ensure the requirements are understood and to allow efficient operation of the establishment.

Opposite: *Note the smaller nursery paddocks closer to the barn.*

Chapter Three
Planning and statutory regulations

Planning permission (UK)

For private use, a stable within a garden and more than 5 m (16 ft) from a dwelling may be allowed without planning permission. However, there are many provisos in the legislation regarding position and height and it is always advisable to have an informal word with the planning officer to confirm this to be the case with the particular development proposed. The diagram on page 24 may help to explain some of the criteria.

Generally, stables, other than those indicated above within the curtilage of a garden and used solely for personal use, require planning permission. This even applies to a single stable or field shelter placed in a paddock. These types of building are not deemed as agricultural and require the same planning permission as any other building. Again, in order to maximise the chance of obtaining planning permission, it is wise to ensure that early informal consultation with the planning officer takes place.

If the proposed building is to be in the grounds of a listed building or in a conservation area, then the work will also require Listed Building Consent which is a separate application.

Stables or other equestrian buildings for a commercial establishment will automatically require planning permission.

As a result of many planning applications for stud farms in the 1980s (and the fundamental necessity for dwellings associated with them on sites which were frequently in the Green Belt or open countryside) many councils have adopted a planning policy specifically related to stud farm development. The planning policy document with which I am currently most familiar, and the one used by many councils, sets out acceptable ratios of horses per acre, horses per stud hand and hence the acceptable number of dwellings that can be justified per acreage.

There is much more to the policy document than the brief synopsis set out above - it includes criteria on which viability can be assessed, references to acceptable locations of buildings and information on ancillary accommodation which might also be approved.

Due to the demise of agriculture in the UK, Whitehall has tried to address the problem and has issued planning

Opposite: *Equestrianism is a pleasant and sympathetic use of the countryside.*

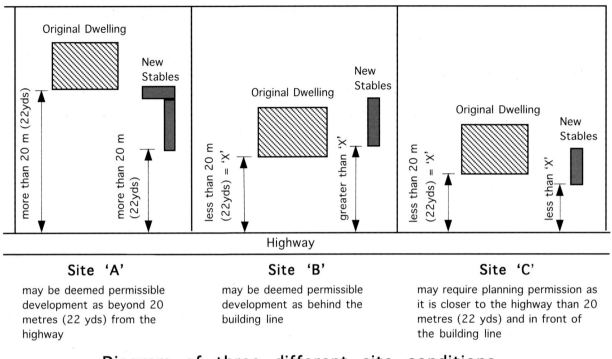

Site 'A'

may be deemed permissible development as beyond 20 metres (22 yds) from the highway

Site 'B'

may be deemed permissible development as behind the building line

Site 'C'

may require planning permission as it is closer to the highway than 20 metres (22 yds) and in front of the building line

Diagram of three different site conditions

Always discuss any individual site informally with planners prior to commencing work

Diagram for planning.

guidelines to planning officers (PPG7) 'The Countryside and the Rural Economy'. These guidelines recognise that the keeping and riding of horses in the country for recreational and leisure purposes is a popular and growing activity and that it helps to provide opportunities for increased employment. Indeed, the labour required to run an equestrian establishment is far greater than that required on an arable farm of comparable size.

In order to mitigate the problems of farmland and farm buildings falling into disuse, the guidelines suggest that planning officers look sympathetically at alternative uses that do not conflict with the countryside in general. Equestrian and related activities are recognised as a compatible use of the countryside as a resource and that they help to sustain the rural economy.

With any commercial development of stables there is often a fundamental need for dwellings associated with the livestock.

On a stud farm there is the critical need for dwelling(s) close to the foaling unit. If existing dwellings are not available or are in inappropriate positions, then planning permission must be sought for new dwellings. This, in planning terms, means that dwellings are recognised as a necessity in relation to this type of equestrian development but that the number and size of dwellings required needs to be justified in terms of the type, size and location of the proposal.

Due to the sensitivity of building in the countryside, it is important that an early site visit takes place with the local planning officer. This not only gives the application a greater chance of success, it also enables the officer to hear the full justification for the development and gives them the opportunity to voice their concerns and for these to be addressed if necessary.

In addition, because of the nature of the development, it is usually worthwhile submitting a report in support of the planning application to maximise the chance of success.

If the development is to be in countryside where planning permission would not normally be allowed and the proposal includes a dwelling, then the local authority, almost without exception, will only grant permission on the basis of what is known as a 'Section 106 Agreement'. This is a legal document drawn up by the local authority and the applicant's solicitor and ties the use of the dwelling(s) solely to persons employed directly on the establishment or directly associated with it. It is usual for the local authority to require signature of this agreement prior to issuing the formal planning permission.

RIGHTS OF WAY

One obstacle that frequently crops up in the planning of a new equine estate is the existence of rights of way. These are extremely undesirable in close proximity to highly strung horses and every effort should be made to design around them.

It may be possible to have a right of way re-routed officially through a planning application but this is becoming increasingly more difficult due to frequent objections from local and national countryside interest groups. On some sites, it may be possible to provide an alternative, more interesting route or it may be possible to provide an alternative, well-sign-posted, unofficial re-routing and this, together with the goodwill of users, can overcome the conflict and dangers associated with the public (and their dogs) near breeding/training horses.

THE LOCAL VERNACULAR

It is usual for stable buildings to be designed in the local vernacular. The form of the building(s) is a reflection of its function and, by tradition, it is true to say that most stables are aesthetically attractive. The addition of clock towers, cupolas, weather vanes, ventilation towers, etc. does a great deal to add visual interest to the building(s) as does the presence of the animals. Also, the maintained neatness of an equestrian development compares very favourably with most agricultural farms and could therefore be argued as an environmental improvement to the rural countryside.

With the many forms of construction and numerous alternative materials now available, it is likely that most concerns of the planning officer can be satisfactorily addressed.

SITING

The major problem in planning terms is usually the siting of the buildings which can lead to a direct conflict between the needs of the establishment to function satisfactorily and the reticence of planners to permit building in the open countryside. Planning officers' general inclination is to refuse permission for anything in open countryside. However, as mentioned previously, government Planning Guidelines have been issued regarding alternative uses for farmland and farm buildings and the need for planners to take a sympathetic attitude should the application be based on a sound business plan.

The need for the countryside to be productive and create employment for its own long term protection is well accepted and changing legislation and methods of farming over the years have shown that attitudes need to be flexible with regard to buildings affected by those changes.

The concerns of the planning officer can also be reduced, to some extent, by the nature of the proposal. If it can be seen that the proposal is a substantial investment and that significant planting will be undertaken as part of the proposal, then the impact on the countryside can be shown to be minimised. It is possible, through judicious siting of the building, together with other actions such as good choice of building materials, semi-mature planting, etc. that the 'newness' of a building can be restricted to just a few months after completion.

Building regulation approval

The local council may also require a building regulation submission for the building works that are proposed. However, this is not a universal approach as some local authorities treat stable buildings as agricultural buildings and therefore deem them exempt from building regulations, while others insist on a full Building Regulation Application together with the compulsory substantial fee.

It is best to ascertain the view of the local authority at an early stage as the stricter legislation under the building regulations may well affect the strength grade of building required which, in turn, will affect the costs.

NATIONAL RIVERS AUTHORITY

A further statutory approval that may be required is from the National Rivers Authority (NRA) if the proposal involves building or diverting drains, ponds or lakes or the discharge of effluent from a sewage disposal system. (See section on drainage, page 52.)

Construction (design & management) regulations - 'CONDAM'

This legislation came into effect in 1995 and puts responsibility on the building owner to ensure that health and safety aspects are in place for the project. The legislation applies to commercial work and requires the building owner to appoint a planning supervisor to ensure all aspects of the legislation are adhered to. The role of the planning supervisor can be undertaken by the owner, the architect, the builder or a specialist planning supervisor.

The Health and Safety Executive must be formally notified of the project at the initial stages before construction and a 'safety file' compiled to take account of all aspects of health and safety during design through to construction, building in use and, eventually, its demolition.

Chapter Four

Accommodation

The nature and size of the establishment will determine what accommodation is required. For a small establishment there may only be a need for a secure tack room and somewhere to store feed, bedding and equipment. On larger establishments the accommodation required may be more specific, with specialist spaces for particular uses.

Boxes

The size of the box will vary according to its use and the size of the animal occupying it. For the larger leisure horse, the hunter, polo pony or racehorse, the normal size is between 14 and 18 sq m (150 and 194 sq ft).

For broodmares the box size is generally increased to about 20 sq m (220 sq ft), while foaling boxes and post-foaling boxes are usually designed at about 23 sq m (250 sq ft).

Although the above suggestions are for square boxes, many people have a preference for rectangular boxes and for these the dimensions should provide an overall area

similar to that stated for a square box.

The minimum height for a box, other than for small pony breeds, should be 3.6 m (12 ft) but this really should be seen as the minimum and 3.8 m ($12\frac{1}{2}$ ft) is preferable as it increases the volume of air in the box which goes a long way to avoiding bad air. (See section on ventilation, page 43.)

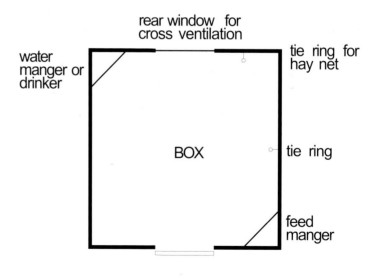

Typical layout of square box.

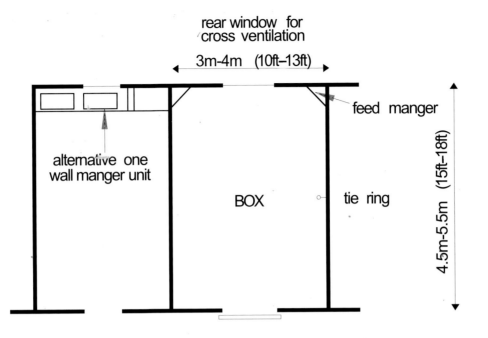

Typical layout of rectangular box.

The natural air currents within the box can be enhanced by the design of the ceiling and by the type of window chosen. (See section on windows, page 61.)

The shape of the ceiling can reduce stagnant air corners and also encourage the natural 'stack effect' or warm air rising from the heat given off by the animal. The warm air currents will rise to the ceiling where they will be pushed along, before cooling and then dropping naturally, giving gentle and draught-free air currents.

The shape of the individual box is less relevant in an American barn. However, if stable boxes in a cellular form are required within an American barn, then the shape of the box again becomes important, perhaps more so, as the ventilation has to be achieved for a box within a box.

To avoid unnecessary physical injury to the animal, care should be taken to avoid any sharp corners or protrusions.

In particular, there should be no arris corners beside the stable door. Should door rollers not be specified then rounded blockwork at the door jambs should be used to prevent an animal from damaging itself on sharp masonry.

The layout for the box will need to provide for feeding and drinking arrangements. In many stables it is normal for auto drinkers to be used and to be sited in the rear corner of the box with the feed manger in one of the front corners where it can be refilled conveniently. The siting of mangers on any project will be at the preference of the owner.

The provision of tie rings and hay racks also needs to be discussed at briefing stage so that individual preferences can be catered for.

UTILITY BOX

In all stables it is an advantage to provide a utility box of about 4 x 4 m (13 x 13 ft). This box may be used for

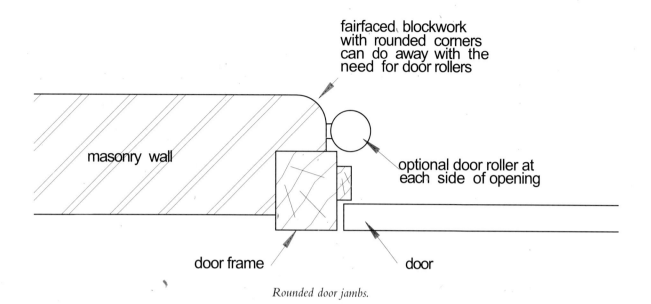

fairfaced blockwork
with rounded corners
can do away with the
need for door rollers

masonry wall

optional door roller at
each side of opening

door frame

door

Rounded door jambs.

washing down, grooming, shoeing, clipping or for the treatment of minor injuries. Where possible, the box should be located centrally to the boxes which it serves. Due to the nature of its use, the utility box should be very easy to wash down and clean.

It is preferable for the utility box to have walls of rubber, at least up to dado height, with a coved rubber skirting and a rubber floor. It will then be possible to clean the surfaces hygienically as these surfaces should be able to withstand frequent washing down. A gully should be set in the centre of the box with the floor laid to fall to the gully. In an American barn-type building at a training stable, the utility box may well be open to the tractor-way, with a tie ring to which the horse is tied while being attended.

WASH DOWN BOX/SPACE

This area is required at competition stables for a horse returning from an arduous exercise session. The box or space needs surfaces able to withstand frequent washing and hosing down and the floor needs to be non-slip

under all conditions. The floor must be laid to fall to a drainage gully and no ponding whatsoever should be allowed.

A tap and hose position should be strategically located for convenience of use but protected so that the horse cannot accidentally injure itself.

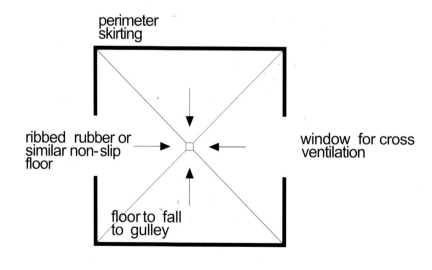

perimeter
skirting

ribbed rubber or
similar non-slip
floor

window for cross
ventilation

floor to fall
to gulley

Wash down box.

In some stable yards, a separate box is provided next to the wash down area which is fitted with banks of infra-red heaters used to dry off the animal and so reduce the risk of it becoming chilled.

The feed store

The feed store should have direct vehicular access for lorries delivering the feed stuffs but, at the same time, be central and convenient for the stable hands to barrow or transfer the food to each stable. Ideally, the feed store should not be close to the manure bunker in order to reduce problems with vermin.

The feed store may also need a space for a linseed boiler with its necessary plumbing and electrical supply and drainage gully.

Water supply in the feed store should be made for both cold water from the mains and also from a storage tank. This will enable the stable to operate in an emergency should the mains water fail. Provision should also be made for hot water, with additional low-level taps for filling buckets.

Ideally, the floor should be concrete with, at the most, a brushed surface to enable easy cleaning and sweeping up. This is essential for hygiene and to avoid encouraging vermin.

Much of the feed stuffs today come ready bagged and these are usually stacked on pallets. However, some owners prefer bulk feed and space is then required for feed bins, augers, baggers, etc.

On larger establishments an oat crusher may also be required, together with a bagger and a storage silo. Although these can be located in the feed store, they are much better located in a separate space where the problem of dust can be more easily controlled.

The sitting up room - foaling unit

This is ideally located centrally between two or four boxes with small, glazed spy holes into the foaling boxes for viewing. The doors into the foaling box should be similar to the traditional half stable door, but with the variation that the bottom door should only be 800 mm (32 in) high. This allows the vet to back the mare up to the lower door for inspection but having protection from injury should the horse kick out.

There should be convenient power points and shelves for the vet to utilise a scanner close to the foaling box door position. It is also of benefit to install a track spot light at high level to light the area where the vet will inspect an animal. With the specification of a tracked spot light system, this will allow adjustment of the light fitting to enable appropriate light direction should the vet be left or right handed.

The room needs to be equipped with a notice board/white board for recording information relating to the various mares that are housed each night. As the foaling period is usually during the winter or early spring, the weather is invariably very cold, so the welfare of the stud hand during their period on duty should be considered. There need to be power points for making coffee etc. and a space for a fridge and possibly a television.

As most foals are born at night, heating the sitting up room to provide comfortable conditions for the supervising staff needs to be considered. Although heating is generally best provided by electric storage heaters, with the vagaries of the British weather it is essential to provide alternative means of boosting heat for changing conditions. This can best be achieved by the use of combi-storage/convector heaters. The combi-heater has

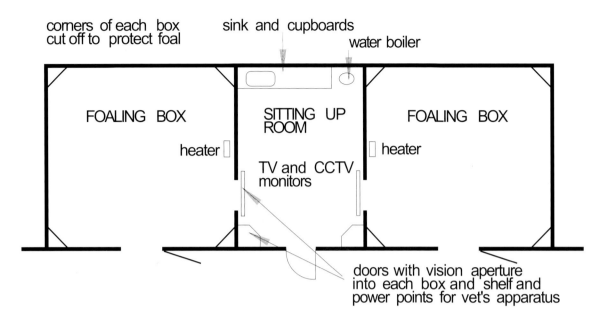

corners of each box
cut off to protect foal

sink and cupboards

water boiler

FOALING BOX

SITTING UP
ROOM

FOALING BOX

heater

heater

TV and CCTV
monitors

doors with vision aperture
into each box and shelf and
power points for vet's apparatus

Sitting up room/foaling box.

the night storage facility, using cheap-rate electricity, but also has flexibility by combining a convection heater which can be used to give instant heat should the temperature drop or the storage heater elements not be fully charged.

Where more valuable mares are foaling, the sitting up room often houses CCTV in order to observe the mares so that extra help can be called if necessary. There may also be a need for a fridge to store drugs.

Another essential piece of equipment is a telephone. Should anything start to go wrong then it is imperative that help can be summoned quickly. Although it is usual to have a fixed phone in the sitting up room, to some extent a mobile phone can serve this requirement – as long as the batteries are not flat!

Observation from the sitting up room to the foaling boxes is often by means of a sliding hatch. This method has proved to be effective over many years.

Experimentation with one-way glass viewing panels into foaling boxes have been made but for this to work satisfactorily the level of lighting in the area from which viewing occurs needs to be lower than in the foaling box. This type of viewing glass panel can, therefore, only be installed beneficially where a non-illuminated lobby is available outside the box.

The simplest solution for discreet viewing is probably a spy hole similar to the type so frequently used in domestic situations for security at the front door.

The crush

This is required at a stud and often on smaller establishments where breeding takes place. Essentially, it is used by the vet to carry out inspection, surgery, etc. while the animal is being restrained from kicking or moving.

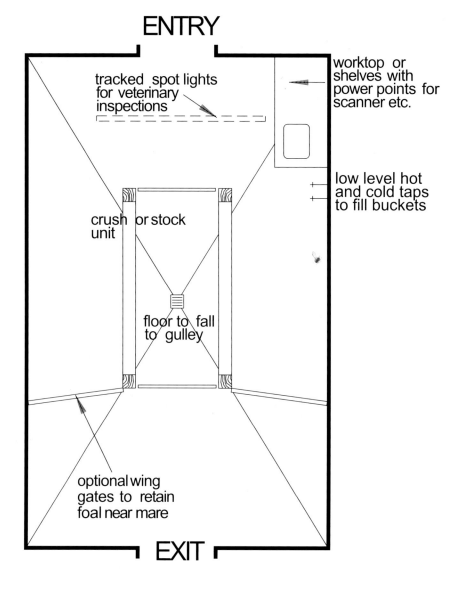

ENTRY

tracked spot lights for veterinary inspections

worktop or shelves with power points for scanner etc.

low level hot and cold taps to fill buckets

crush or stock unit

floor to fall to gulley

optional wing gates to retain foal near mare

EXIT

Diagram of a crush.

Typical crush or stocks.

The stock unit itself is a proprietary item, supplied and bolted in place. It is possible to have parts of the stock unit made to measure so that the wing gates provide a physical separation between mare and foal and allow veterinary examinations to proceed unhindered.

The crush's use dictates that hygiene is of great

importance and this should be reflected in the finishes that are chosen. All surfaces need to be steam cleanable and the floor needs to be non-slip, impervious and puddle free. A rubber floor with sealed welded joints or a resilient, *in situ* floor, complete with coved skirting, has proved to be ideal.

There should be adequate power points with shelf facilities close at hand for the vet. Frequently, spot lights are provided to give better illumination. Cupboard storage facilities, one of which should be lockable, and a sink with hot and cold water, with bucket-filling capability, should also be provided.

It has been established that an animal tends to be comforted by heat and therefore it is sensible to install sets of infra-red lamps which can be switched on while the horse is undergoing examination and likely to be in an apprehensive state.

Vet's room

If a specific vet's room is incorporated, then it should have many of the facilities already mentioned for the crush, i.e.

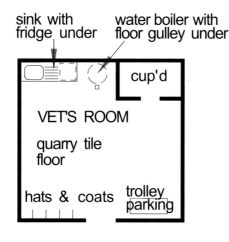

Vet's room.

cupboard storage, sink, hot and cold water. It should also have a fridge for storage of drugs.

The floor finish should be quarry tiles or a similar, impervious non-slip finish. Preferably, the floor level in the vet's room should be the same as that of the adjacent rooms and the outside apron as, on larger establishments, a trolley is often used to take medication from box to box.

Tack room

This is an essential room on all equine establishments. The tack itself is very expensive and is frequently the object of theft. The siting of the tack room is, therefore, important as are the security measures that should be taken.

In the construction of the tack room practical measures should be taken to make theft more difficult. Firstly, the layout should try to eliminate any possible entry points. Access should be restricted to one door only, which should be of solid construction. The ironmongery should be specified as security standard with a minimum of two locks. Often, a solid door is specified but intruders can lever the door from the frame so it is crucial to ensure that the door frame is also of a substantial size and made of robust timber.

If possible, a rectangular shape should be used for the room as this will provide a larger wall to floor ratio, thereby increasing the amount of wall space available for storage of tack.

If there are any windows, these should be located at a high level to allow maximum wall space below for hanging equipment. Most importantly, they need to be fitted internally with substantial security grilles.

Statistics show that many tack room break-ins occur through the ceiling/roof construction. A very inexpensive and effective way to provide security to the ceiling

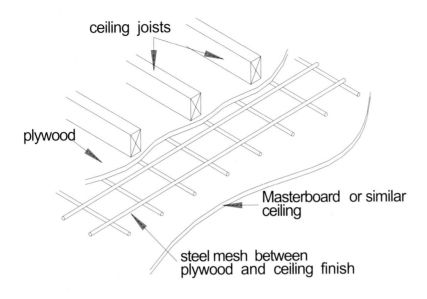

Tack room ceiling.

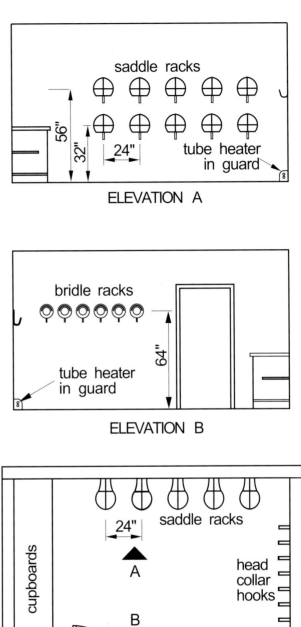

construction is to form the ceiling of a sandwich layer of steel mesh reinforcement. If the ceiling is constructed from plywood sheets screwed to the ceiling joists with the steel mesh below and finished on the room side with a fireproof board such as 'masterboard', a thief will have great difficulty in gaining access.

If the tack room shell is soundly constructed, then security can best be enhanced by the installation of a security detector and alarm. These are relatively inexpensive to install and, with prominently displayed notices advertising the fact that the tack room has an alarm system, should provide security from all but the most determined thief.

To keep the tack in prime condition it is necessary to have good ventilation following the prerequisite of suitable background heating. The heating needs to be held at a relatively constant temperature to protect the leather without drying it out, but with good ventilation to expel any moist air. Care should be taken in the siting of heating appliances which may require guards to prevent

Tack room.

leather from direct contact as overheating of the tack is as detrimental as no heat at all.

Adequate quantities of tack hooks, saddle racks, etc. should be installed and these need to be agreed early on to ensure sufficient space is provided. It is common for the tack room also to be used for cleaning the tack, therefore a sink with hot and cold water is necessary, together with some cupboard space for the cleaning utensils and materials.

The floor should be durable and easy to clean. One of the best flooring materials is quarry tiles which, if specified with a coved skirting, can produce an easy-clean, waterproof and long-lasting finish.

Blanket room

This is a facility that is often forgotten, although on small establishments, the tack room will double as a blanket room. It is used to dry out blankets etc. and is essential in a yard where there are many animals that are regularly blanketed and exercised. A damp or wet blanket is likely to considerably increase the chance of an animal catching a cold, chill or viral infection and be unavailable for competition.

The blanket room requires racking on which to hang the blankets and good insulation in order to cut down on energy consumption. The heating should be at low level and floor-mounted radiant tubes lend themselves well to this use.

The floor need only be concrete, although quarry tiles are also suitable and easier to clean.

In order to achieve optimum performance from the heat input, it is necessary to install some degree of high-level cross-ventilation to remove the humidity in the air which has been extracted from the wet blankets. In large drying rooms, it will be necessary to install a mechanical extractor to take away this moist air.

In addition to blanket racks fixed to the wall, there may be a requirement for blanket storage, although dry blankets are best kept in the tack room.

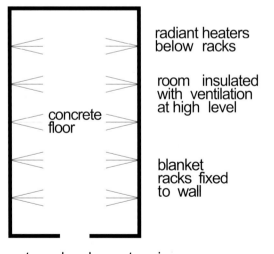

Diagram of a blanket room.

radiant heaters below racks

room insulated with ventilation at high level

concrete floor

blanket racks fixed to wall

rectangular shape to give maximum wall space

Isolation box

On establishments of any size there will be a need for isolation boxes. These will be used both for horses that have an infection and horses newly arrived from another establishment.

In its simplest form, the isolation box can be separated from other boxes by ancillary accommodation (see diagram on page 7). On larger premises isolation boxes will be required well away from the normal boxes and may even be located on a separate part of the estate, complete with individual isolation paddocks and perhaps a dedicated indoor exercise barn.

By necessity, the isolation boxes need to be accessed

from a route not frequented by staff and other animals. Often, nominated staff are delegated to look after the isolated horses in order to minimise the risk of spreading infection.

Solarium

Generally, the solarium is used to dry an animal although it is often also used for therapeutic purposes to promote the healing of an injured or sick animal or to help an animal recover from inflammation.

The space required for a solarium unit is about 2.5 x 1.5 m (8 x 5 ft) so it can be located quite comfortably in a spare box or part of the crush.

Exercise barn

This can be a space varying between 12 and 16 metres square (129-172 feet square) depending on its use. If it is to be used solely for turning out a sick animal in a breeding barn, the smaller size will be adequate, but if it is also to serve for lungeing, then the larger size should be allowed.

The larger size may also be necessary if the intention is to turn out wintering yearlings or young stock. However, if this is the intention, some form of low-level barred opening within the external walls of the building should be included in order that an inquisitive animal can see out and observe activity in the yard. Without an opportunity to see the outside world, there is an increased likelihood of the animal indulging in such vices as crib biting around the doors, and other unwanted behaviour.

It is quite sufficient for the walls to be of fairfaced blockwork, although at low level, up to approximately

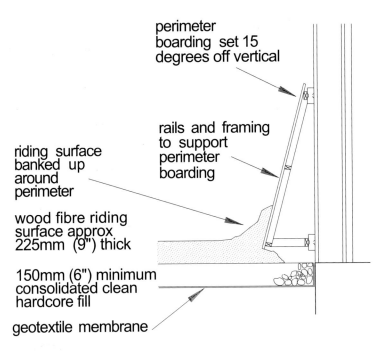

riding surface banked up around perimeter

perimeter boarding set 15 degrees off vertical

rails and framing to support perimeter boarding

wood fibre riding surface approx 225mm (9") thick

150mm (6") minimum consolidated clean hardcore fill

geotextile membrane

Wall boarding to indoor school.

2 m (6.5 ft) it is preferable to have angled boarding. It is certainly essential to round off all the corners and to design out or pad any protrusions such as door jambs.

Where padding is used, then the foam needs to be of upholstery quality, with the casing of a material that cannot be split by chewing or kicking. Rubber sheeting (5 mm) is ideal, while reinforced proprietary membranes are a good alternative and much less costly.

The flooring finish in this area will be dependent on use and the preference of the owner. Products such as tan, wood chip, bark, fibre sand or Pasada will all dry out and the facility to damp the surface down to prevent dust is essential, therefore a convenient standpipe needs to be provided outside, together with a suitable length of hose. On larger or commercial premises, installation of a sprinkler system may be desirable.

Should the space also be used for covering, then consideration should be given to Equitrack as this product has lower dusting qualities.

Provision should be made for natural lighting and this is best achieved by roof lights which will, if evenly and frequently spaced out, ensure an even spread of light.

Artificial lighting is mentioned in more detail in the section on lighting, (page 48) but will generally be a choice of fluorescent, sodium or mercury. Both sodium and mercury lights require a period of time to warm up before they reach full brightness and, for safety reasons, the lamps should be fitted with a wire cage or diffuser to reduce the dangers in the event of a bulb breakage. Fluorescent tubes are economic to install and, for infrequent use, are the best option.

It will be necessary to provide a 13 amp waterproof point somewhere in close proximity to the exercise area. However, care should be taken to ensure that such fixtures do not protrude into the working area.

Ventilation is extremely important and, with the high roof level within this type of space, there is the opportunity to provide an abundance of ventilation. This should be at high level and can be achieved either by groups of louvres or, preferably, by perimeter Yorkshire boarding. Yorkshire boarding with gaps of 10-25 mm is ideal, however, it is equally important that excessive gaps are not left between the boards as rain and snow penetration can become a problem. To reduce the risk of driving rain penetrating the external envelope, it is possible to tack plastic gauze mesh to the inner face of the boarding (see illustration on page 48).

Covering barn

On a stud farm that stands stallions there will be the need for a covering barn. The barn needs to be a minimum of 10 x 10 m (33 x 33 ft) with smooth walls up to a height of 2 m (6$\frac{1}{2}$ ft). On small establishments the walls may be boarded and may be cushioned by the addition of coco matting. On larger establishments the padding is often provided by PVC-covered padded panels hung or secured to the walls.

As in an exercise barn all door jambs and other protrusions need to be well padded.

The flooring is usually composed of loose fill to give a cushioning effect and to help with grip. One of the best finishes, Equitrak, has all the best characteristics required and is non-dusting and hygienic in use.

Attached to the covering barn there could be a teaser box. This box should have a top door only, which opens on to the covering barn with the facility to be closed off after the mare has been presented. It is essential that this top door is sliding and not hinged so that there are no protrusions into the covering barn.

In addition to the teaser box there may be a requirement for a teaser board/gate. This should be hinged in a manner that enables it to be hinged away when not in use to provide a totally clear barn space when the actual covering is to be carried out.

Hay and straw barn

The size of this building will depend on the number of boxes and whether smaller hay and straw stores are also located in each of the barns/yards.

The hay and straw barn needs to be a minimum of 6.3 m (21 ft) high to enable access by a fully laden delivery lorry. The building should be in bay construction so that hay and straw can be stored apart.

The most suitable flooring is concrete, with the finished level some 50 mm (2 in) above the general outside level in order to prevent flooding and damage to the bottom layer of stored material. Often the bottom layer of bales is stored on pallets so that air can circulate and keep the material in good condition.

Ventilation should be provided around the barn, particularly at higher levels where a build up of heat is more likely to occur. Ventilation should be achieved without allowing the ingress of rain which could damage the stored material. The roof should also allow ventilation and this is best achieved at the ridge as any heat build up will naturally rise.

The lower part of the barn walls should be of masonry construction which is noncombustible and vermin-proof.

The barn should be located close to where the heavy delivery lorries will be entering the site in order to reduce the area of strengthened road construction required. The barn should also be located for convenient access and use by the stable staff but, at the same time, well away from stables or other buildings which could become vulnerable in the case of a fire.

When choosing the site it is well worthwhile bearing in mind the prevailing rain-bearing winds which, in the UK, are south-westerly. To reduce the loss of prime forage and bedding, the open side of the barn should not face south west.

If the layout allows, every effort should be made to locate the hay and straw barn away from the manure bunker and certainly on the windward side of the manure bunker in order to reduce the likelihood of fungal spore contamination.

Lastly, the hay and straw barn is a high-risk fire area and, although a major fire could not be tackled, it is essential to have several water/gas extinguishers located in an easily accessible place so that a minor incident could be tackled and, hopefully, extinguished.

Garaging for vehicles

For the owner with only a few ponies or horses, a single- or two-horse trailer is probably the most common mode of transporting the animals. The size of a two-horse trailer is usually about 2.7 m high x 2.3 m wide x 4.5 m long (9 x 7$\frac{1}{2}$ x 15 ft). This is too high and too wide for a domestic garage and, frequently, the trailer is left out in the open.

As with a motor car, many experts advise that the vehicle should not be garaged but is best left under a roof or car port-type shelter where it is protected from rainfall and can dry out. Allowing the trailer to dry out is particularly important as it is generally the timber floor that is the first item to rot due to the effect of horse droppings and urine.

Should a garage or car port space be required, it will need a clear height of 2.7 m (9 ft).

For a motorised horse transporter the height required for storing under cover is generally a maximum of 3.6 m (12 ft), although individual transporters vary and should be checked specifically for each project.

The disadvantage of leaving a horsebox or horse trailer ungaraged is the likelihood of theft. This is becoming an increasing problem and measures ought to be taken to protect the equipment. Certainly, for a towing trailer it is essential to use a lockable security device over the tow hitch to make it difficult for a thief to hitch up to their own vehicle. Tow hitch security devices are readily available from auto parts dealers and can save a lot of frustration and inconvenience.

Indoor school

The minimum size for an indoor school is 40 x 20 m (44 x 22 yd) which is the standard dressage arena, laid out in

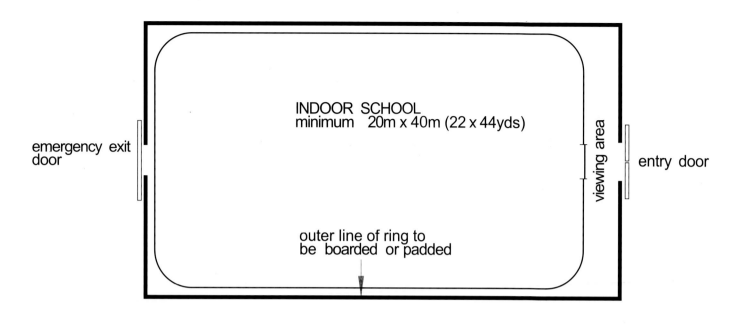

Indoor school.

the form shown above. While building an indoor school, it will cost very little extra to create a larger space than the minimum specified and this will allow many more options for its use including facilities such as viewing areas.

A portal-framed steel structure is the easiest and cheapest way to achieve an indoor school. The steel portal frames are usually spaced at about 5.5-6 m (18-20 ft) centres each erected off a concrete pad foundation. A minimum internal clear height at the eaves of 4 m (13 ft) is required and this figure needs to be increased with the size of the building, otherwise an overbearing effect will be created. Remember also that at the joint of roof and wall the steel frame will be thicker and lower and this will create the visual impression of a lower roof height.

The roof will normally be at a pitch of between 12 and 15 degrees due to its larger span, and the roof covering should be regularly spaced with rooflights to allow even daylight without bright or shadowed areas. The roof of an

indoor school need not be insulated as the animal is not in the building the whole time. However, insulated roof panels will reduce the noise levels from rain and hail if this is felt likely to be a problem, for example if an instructor's voice is to be heard.

The walls of this type of building should generally be of industrial metal sheet cladding, although the outside could be faced with brickwork or timber slats where appearance is of importance. The cladding should be designed to allow considerable ventilation as the animal will be in working mode in the school and will be giving off a high degree of moisture. High levels of ventilation can be readily achieved with Yorkshire boarding or similar ventilators such as louvres. The ventilation is required all round the perimeter of an indoor school to ensure that there will be no problems with condensation.

Lighting for the area should be bright and even in order not to dazzle horse or rider. It should also be installed as high as possible in order to reduce glare. Low-energy sodium or mercury vapour lights are ideal but do require a short warm up time before they achieve full brightness. The advantage of these types of light is their low running costs.

The internal surface material of the roof should be light to avoid great disparity between the ceiling and the rooflights. A light-coloured ceiling will also help to reflect both daylight and artificial light to give a more even lighting level.

The range of materials available for the floor finish has increased considerably in recent years, with many specialist products coming on to the market. Non-specialist finishes include wood chip, bark, tan and sand. A few require little maintenance and are dust-free, while most dry out rapidly and dust up and therefore require frequent watering down with a hose or sprinkler system. If one of these drier types of loose finish is intended, then serious consideration should be

given to installing a watering facility.

The low-level internal walling of the school (below 1.8 m [6 ft]) should be boarded. This should be constructed at an angle to prevent riders from being dragged off should the horse come too close to the wall. Plywood is a very suitable material for this type of lining and can easily be fixed to softwood framing. As horses will be moving in the indoor school at speed, it is essential that all protrusions are avoided. If this is not possible then it is essential that all remaining protrusions are thickly padded, including the door jambs and structural steel frames. The padding should be a dense upholstery-type foam with a covering that can be easily cleaned down.

Some owners may require a viewing area within the school. This can be achieved by raising the floor level so that viewing takes place above the internal timber lining.

The site needs to be carefully selected as a sloping site can lead to considerable excavation and filling for such a

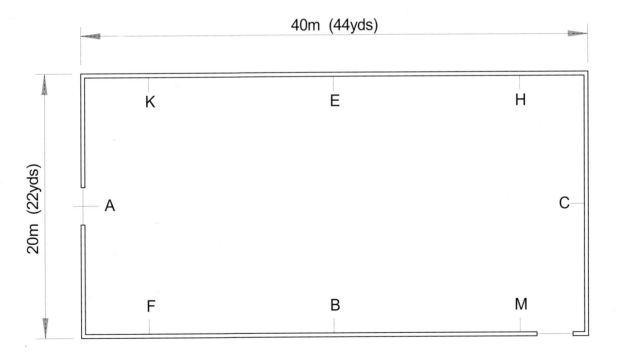

Arena.

large building. The slope of the surrounding land also needs to be considered in terms of where the surface water will flow. Excess surface water from the surrounding areas should not fall toward the building. If this is unavoidable, then a French drain will need to be installed around the building to resolve the problem.

As the building has a large floor area the roof will, consequently, be high, which can present problems for maintenance and cleaning of the light fittings. The most convenient method will generally be by tower scaffold or cherry picker, both of which can be hired from most machinery hire shops.

Outdoor arena or manège

The site for the arena should be considered in terms of the topography, soil composition, adjacent land uses and future expansion plans. Ideally, the site should be well drained, slightly sloping and in a position where it can be enlarged if required should future needs dictate. The site should have no distractions to the horse and rider, such as recreation grounds, adjacent highways or footpaths.

The minimum recommended size for a small outdoor arena is 40 x 20 m (44 x 22 yd) laid out for dressage. This size also allows most ponies and horses to turn comfortably and undertake simple jumping safely. For more serious jumping, the arena size will need to be increased.

The perimeter fencing should be paddock-type three- or four-rail with well-firmed-in posts and a kick rail at low level around the perimeter to prevent the riding surface from being lost outside the arena. The surface finish will probably be one of those mentioned for the indoor school but for external use it will be essential to provide some form of drainage in the construction.

Ideally, the arena should be sited on land that is well

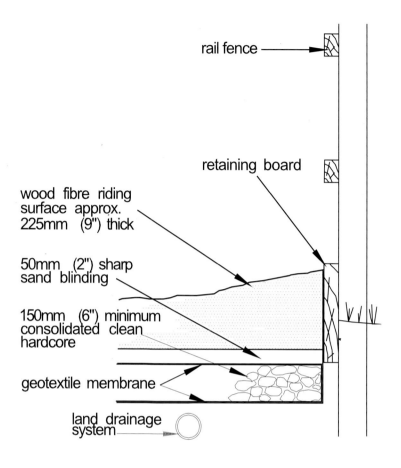

rail fence

retaining board

wood fibre riding surface approx. 225mm (9") thick

50mm (2") sharp sand blinding

150mm (6") minimum consolidated clean hardcore

geotextile membrane

land drainage system

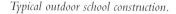

Typical outdoor school construction.

drained with a marginal slope. If this can be achieved, the base course may also become the drainage layer if suitable material is used.

If the outdoor school has been cut into the slope of the ground it is crucial to provide drainage around the perimeter, particularly on the sides of the arena that are 'cut in', in order to prevent surface rainwater from the surrounding area draining down on to the arena and making it boggy and unusable. A French drain may be found suitable for this purpose.

As with the foundation of a building, it is essential to start off the arena construction with a good base. For an outdoor arena the prepared ground should first be covered with a geotextile membrane. The geotextile membrane is very important as it will allow water to pass through but will prevent the loss of aggregate into the ground or fines back into the aggregate. It also helps to retain a firm base for the ride. A clean base layer is also essential to good drainage.

If the site chosen for the arena tends to be wet then additional drainage precautions need to be taken. On ground prone to holding water, it is advisable to install a system of land drains below the drainage layer, with the drainage pipes being taken to a soakaway or water course.

The hardcore base for the arena should be clean, crushed limestone or, better still, MOT 1 aggregate, both of which should be well rolled in and consolidated. A timber retaining board fixed to the perimeter fencing will prevent overspill of the ride surface on to the surrounding ground.

The surface of the arena may be a proprietary material or sharp sand, woodchip or bark. The depth of the surface finish will depend on the material chosen but will be between 125 and 250 mm (5-10 in).

If bark or woodchip is used it is worthwhile laying a second geotextile membrane over the hardcore, ensuring that all joints are secured, topping this with 50 mm (2 in) of sharp sand and finished with 175 mm (7 in) of bark. This form of construction will drain well and ensure easy removal of old, worn-out surfacing.

The outdoor arena, like the indoor school, will require damping down occasionally in order to prevent dust so a standpipe needs to be located in close proximity.

Chapter Five
Services

Ventilation in boxes

Probably the most important aspect of equine accommodation is the need for adequate and proper ventilation. It is now recognised that a far higher level of ventilation is required in a box than had previously been considered necessary.

A horse's health and performance can be substantially impaired by infection resulting from poor ventilation or stale air. Research by Andrew Clarke MRCVS at Bristol University has shown that horses are no different from humans with regard to the effects of poor air. Respiratory problems and mucus retention are exacerbated by poor or polluted air, just as human asthmatics suffer more in polluted air.

Research on cattle buildings has shown that high humidity and low temperature, resulting in a damp environment, in turn leads to the spread of droplet infection. If high humidity and high temperature conditions are provided, the animals suffer from a high metabolic rate and poor food conversion.

Increased ventilation in itself will not reduce the risk of air-borne infection but it will help to dilute any infection present in the air and will also help to remove damp, stale air. The ideal environmental conditions are frequent air changes with clean fresh air but without introducing draughts.

Good ventilation alone will not provide the best environmental conditions if the structure is not also designed to help, therefore the building needs to be carefully thought out to achieve optimum performance.

The natural air movement within a box is generally by:

- stack effect
- aspiration
- wind effect.

STACK EFFECT
This is the movement of warm air generated by heat given off by the animal. The rising air currents induce a circular air movement within the box.

ASPIRATION
This is the effect of wind outside the box passing over the

building and sucking out air from the box as it passes over.

WIND EFFECT

This is the direct effect of air entering and passing through the box. This can have the greatest impact on the ventilation rate within a box but should not be relied on as the sole source of ventilation as, on a windless day, the box would not be adequately ventilated.

In order to achieve a high degree of ventilation, it is necessary to know what the air movement within the box will be.

Prevailing weather conditions have the most significant effect on the ventilation rate in a stable. On a windy day in a traditional yard with the box top door open, air change rates could be in the order of tens per hour. In extreme cold and windy conditions, this rate would require the top door of the box to be closed.

Conversely, on a still day the ventilation rate could be virtually nil apart from aspiration and this is where the design of the box can enhance the ventilation and provide better conditions for the horse.

Air movement can be encouraged by the shape of the

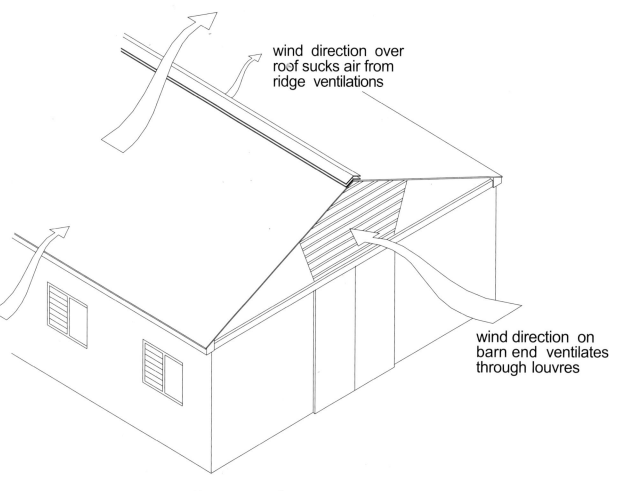

wind direction over roof sucks air from ridge ventilations

wind direction on barn end ventilates through louvres

Air movement over barn.

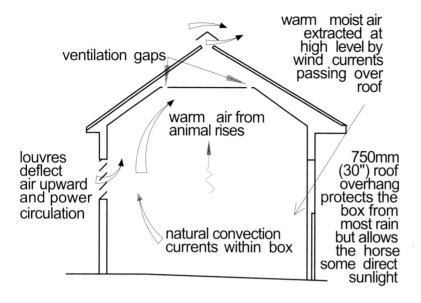

ventilation gaps

warm moist air extracted at high level by wind currents passing over roof

warm air from animal rises

louvres deflect air upward and power circulation

750mm (30") roof overhang protects the box from most rain but allows the horse some direct sunlight

natural convection currents within box

Air movement in traditional box.

roof and ceiling and also by the materials used in construction. Solid masonry walls tend to be cool and, in summer, induce cool downward air currents round the perimeter of the box, creating a comfortable environment. Boxes constructed of timber will become particularly hot in summer especially the highest parts of the box near the roof and excellent, high–level ventilation becomes a necessity.

For the purposes of calculating ventilation rates, it should be assumed that the top door to the box is closed.

To find out the natural air currents within a box a smoke device can be used to establish the air movement and the air extraction.

Fresh air should be available to the horse at all times. As a rule, the optimum number of air changes per hour should be between three and ten. Below three, the air can become stale, and, above ten, the problems of 'chill factor' and draughts become more significant.

For a typical box of 3.6 x 3.6 x 3.3 m (12 x 12 x 11 ft) high, the air volume would be 43 cu m (1584 cu ft). For

three air changes this is approximately 130 cu m (4750 cu ft) of natural ventilation per hour. The design of the ventilation for the box should, *as a minimum*, be based on this data and result in an even, controllable air movement.

As an example the following formula will give the total area of ventilation inlets required for a box. Calculation is in imperial units:

$$S = \text{air volume of box (cu ft)}$$
$$V = \text{velocity of air (feet per second)}$$
$$T = \text{time for air changes in seconds}$$
$$A = \text{area of outlets required (sq ft)}$$

$$A = \frac{S}{V \times T}$$

For the purposes of calculation assume a wind speed of 2 ft per second.

An average box size would be 1584 cu ft with a minimum air change rate of 3 per hour. An air change rate of 3 per hour is 1 air change each 1200 seconds.

$$A = \frac{1584}{2 \times 1200} = 0.66 \text{ sq ft. or } 95 \text{ sq inches.}$$

It is worth noting that it is pointless having plenty of air inlets if there is nowhere for the stale air to go. The important factor in the design of ventilation is to balance the size of air inlets with the air outlets and to encourage air movement, with air inlets and outlets at different levels.

This can be achieved in many ways. However, in all cases it is essential to avoid draughts. As with a human athlete, draughts can cause stiffness in the muscles and an animal is no different. Stiff muscles can, in turn, be the cause of pulled muscles and result in an unwelcome period out of action.

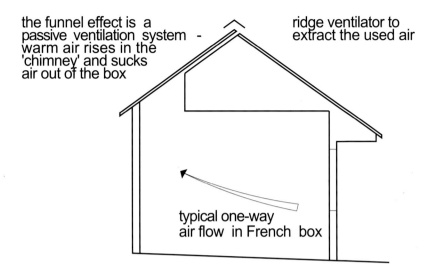

the funnel effect is a passive ventilation system - warm air rises in the 'chimney' and sucks air out of the box

ridge ventilator to extract the used air

typical one-way air flow in French box

Ventilation in a typical French box.

Ventilation in an American barn is not quite so critical in terms of air change rates due to the volume formed by the barn structure. However, continuous fresh air must be available to all boxes at all times. The large air volume of the barn shape is conducive to creating a positive air flow that will avoid stale spots. This can be negated if the roof is not well insulated so it is essential that the roof is insulated to avoid cold, damp, down draughts.

If the roof is well insulated, the heat given off by the animals will induce natural rising air convection which, in turn, can be exaggerated by directed eaves ventilators and by the use of ridge vents.

The presence of natural wind currents over the stable can also exaggerate the air movement within the stable without causing draughts. This is similar in effect to the wind passing over the wing of an aircraft, causing uplift. Over the roof of a building the wind causes high and low pressure areas. These vortices can be used to help to suck air from the ridge vents, increasing the air extraction from the box. In effect, this is forced air extraction without the need to rely on mechanical apparatus.

In an American barn, if the prevailing wind is along the ridge line, it is preferable to introduce apex louvres at the gable ends over the tractor-ways. This will ensure that good ventilation is achieved whatever the wind direction.

Some owners are so concerned about the risk of cross-infection of stock that they insist on each stable having its own individual cross-flow of air with the party walls between boxes totally separating each box. This can only be effectively achieved in a traditional yard arrangement.

Coughing or infected animals can soon infect their neighbours. The ventilation and/or separation of air between boxes can be a significant help in reducing the chance of spread of infection.

Poor ventilation is only one aspect of the spread of infectious diseases. Another source of respiratory infection is dust particles from bedding and hay. Hay and straw can contain a large incidence of fungal spores which can themselves be a source of infection. It is usually recommended that hay should be left in the stable at below shoulder height so that any dust disturbed is likely to fall down and away from the animal's breathing passages instead of over its face and eyes, which often happens with traditional hay racks.

One point which should be mentioned is that no natural ventilation system will perform in the same way in all weather conditions. The outside wind speed will have a large bearing on the ventilation rate within the box and, to an extent, the degree of ventilation will also be governed by the aspect of the boxes/building. Obviously, a more consistent and adequate natural ventilation system will be achieved in an American barn where there is a much larger air volume.

It is possible to supplement the natural ventilation with mechanical installations but this is costly both in terms of capital outlay and maintenance. Reliance on a mechanical system is inadvisable and should be unnecessary if adequate provision is made at design stage.

Opposite: above *A ridge vent on old boxes providing better ventilation than is found on many new boxes.*
below *Old stables well ventilated by lantern vent.*

The management of a stable will also have some impact on the air quality within the box. One example is urine in a stable held within the bedding or in some types of flooring.

Retention of urine within the box will give off ammonia (a chemical irritant). This irritates the respiratory passages of a horse to the extent that it is more susceptible to infection. If the animal is subject to a source of bacteria or other infectious agent, it is much more likely to become infected if its respiratory passages are already inflamed.

Some stable floors have resilient, loose-laid tiles that butt together and can be washed down. These tiles need to be removed at regular intervals and both the tiles and the box thoroughly cleaned and disinfected. Although chemicals can be used daily to neutralise ammonia, it would seem more sensible to specify a monolithic floor which is stuck down and has no cracks or crevices to hold urine or allow bacteria build up.

VENTILATION IN EXERCISE BARNS AND SIMILAR SPACES

In an exercise barn, lungeing ring or schooling ring the animal at exercise requires a much higher rate of fresh air ventilation than in a stable where it is at rest.

The added heat and perspiration given off in an exercise or lungeing ring require the levels of ventilation to be dramatically increased. One of the most effective forms of ventilation for this type of use is 'hit and miss' Yorkshire boarding. This can be either single layer, with boards separated by 12-25 mm (0.5-1 in) gaps for ventilation or, alternatively, the Yorkshire boarding can be specified in two layers with the inner layer staggered to cover the gaps in the outer layer.

This second method has the advantage of giving excellent ventilation while reducing direct draughts. It also reduces the chances of snow or rain penetration.

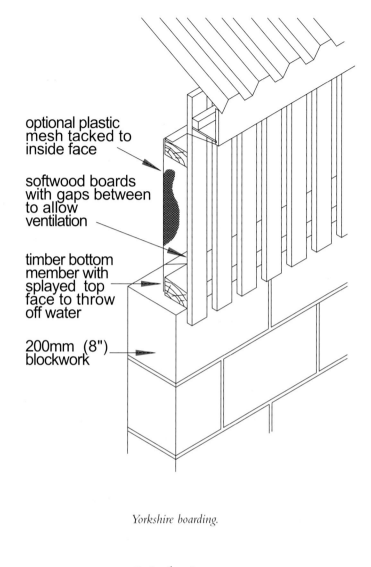

optional plastic mesh tacked to inside face

softwood boards with gaps between to allow ventilation

timber bottom member with splayed top face to throw off water

200mm (8") blockwork

Yorkshire boarding.

Lighting

Generally, lighting in boxes is by fluorescent fittings which need to be moisture-resistant and able to withstand the frequent steam cleaning that has to take place in a stable. They also need to be specified with unbreakable diffusers such as polycarbonate. There are three basic starter mechanisms for fluorescent fittings and the more expensive electronic starter is preferable as this eliminates the noise and flicker on start up which can startle edgy horses.

For an average size 4 x 4 m (13 x 13 ft) box, a twin 1.8 m (6 ft) fluorescent with moisture proof fitting will give a lighting level of 250 lux. For general use 200 lux should be sufficient, with increased task lighting where special jobs are undertaken, such as in the crush. Special task lighting can be achieved by the installation of spot lights.

The installation of a small tungsten fitting as well as the fluorescent light in the stable enables the stable hand or security man to check the horse at night without the severity of a very bright fluorescent light startling the animal. However, this is a bonus and not essential.

The yard should be provided with normal tungsten bulkhead fittings regularly spaced under the roof overhang to provide safe passage around the yard to check the animal at night.

In exercise barns, indoor arenas or even American barns where the lights are likely to be on for a long period of time, consideration should be given to sodium or mercury vapour lights. Their initial cost is higher but substantial savings can be made on lower running costs and less frequent replacement of bulbs.

Should the sodium or mercury lamp be used in any space associated with horses, the lamp must be shielded by a diffuser. Although the lamps have a very long life, the diffuser will ensure that a broken bulb or filament cannot drop down and startle a horse or, indeed, become a fire hazard by dropping on to any combustible floor material or bedding.

Much of this book is based on achieving buildings designed to cater for the natural needs of the animal. However, with the rules of racing determining that a horse has a birthday every January 1st with an 11-month gestation period, it becomes necessary to mate the animals out of their natural season. This is an area where research

and modern technology have considerably helped the commercial stud.

Modern advances with light technology have enabled the production of lights that emit light in wavelengths very close to those of ordinary daylight. The use of daylight fittings switched by a timer can simulate a longer day which, in turn, can stimulate the mare in her cycle and offer the chance of early conception and hence the benefit of the early foal so valuable to the commercial market. The lighting level for this type of use may well need to be increased to 1,000 lux at the lighting plane as the level of illumination is of equal importance as the type of light waves in stimulating the natural breeding metabolism.

The manager on one particular stud where artificial daylight tubes have been specified was amazed and delighted by achieving 100 per cent conception rate of his barren mares at a very early date. The success was put down in part to the effectiveness of the lighting system.

As well as the benefit of bringing mares into season earlier by the higher light levels installed, the same sort of physiological change can be achieved with stallions. Higher lighting levels have been shown to increase the fertility/sperm count of the stallion. This is little more than could be expected as, in the wild, the procreation instincts of the horse rise in spring due to the lighter, warmer and longer days.

In a training stable, lighting levels can have a similar effect in that higher levels of light can help to bring an animal into its coat earlier. Daylight and sunlight are essential to most mammals. Sunlight is a source of vitamin D which is known to affect the pituitary gland which in turn, controls growth and bodily functions. In particular, it affects the alertness of the animal. Conversely, a dark stable has the effect of making the animal sleepy, an undesirable trait in an equine athlete.

Exterior lighting around a yard or building can illuminate the immediate surroundings for access.

However, it is more practical in a working yard or on the exterior of an American barn to use halogen floodlights which are activated via movement detectors. These also act as a security measure and provide excellent levels of lighting, with a single fitting illuminating a large area.

Water

The majority of stables now use automatic drinkers, although some still prefer to use traditional drinking mangers or buckets so that the water intake of the animal can be monitored. Modern auto drinkers are generally robust and trouble free, with the biggest problem being the routing of the pipes.

On box designs where there is a one-wall drinking and feeding arrangement the pipe work insulation, protection and accessibility is much more easily resolved by running the pipe work in the manger void, with access panels in each box which can also house the individual isolating valves.

The route of the pipe work around the building should be given careful consideration. It is essential that pipes are not in a position where a curious horse can cause damage to the pipes or insulation, but they should be positioned where they can easily be maintained and repaired without major disruption.

To avoid frozen water-supply pipes, it is common practice to install trace heating to water pipework within equine buildings. Although preferable, trace heating is not a necessity and good insulation will be adequate in all except the most severe periods of frost. To some extent, the routing of the pipework can also help to reduce the likelihood of frozen pipes, especially if the pipework is kept away from the external walls and cold draughts.

If trace heating is used it should be remembered that the

Typical enamelled auto drinker;
note the protection of the water supply.

horse is very susceptible to electrical shocks, even at low voltages. If there is a chance that the horse can bite a pipe or insulation, then it surely will. With careful thought it is usually fairly easy to route trace-heated pipes out of reach of the horse.

It is possible to run the water pipes below ground to rise in the corner of each box with the pipe between the floor and the water point, trace heated and cased in. The problem with this solution is that there are then many pipe joints below ground and these are potential leakage points. A leak can be expensive to investigate and repair, apart from the actual cost of the wasted water and possible associated damage caused by the water leakage. A more favourable solution is to run the pipe work at high level

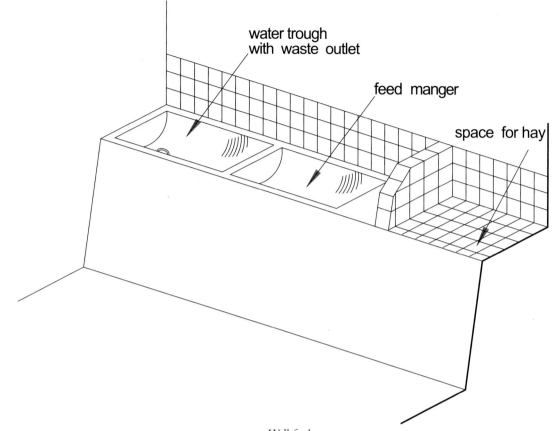

water trough
with waste outlet

feed manger

space for hay

Wall feeder.

where it can be trace heated and protected and is readily accessible.

When considering the layout for the water services, it is necessary to size the pipes in order to provide sufficient water for a fire hose point at some location within each yard. It will also be necessary to locate convenient stop valve positions, air vent joints and flushing points for the whole establishment to enable easy plumbing repair or maintenance work.

Research into cattle breeding has shown that the presence of nitrates in the water supply has a retarding effect on the growth of an animal. It is possible that the same negative effect applies to horses. Apart from the effect on growth, the presence of 'pollutants' is accepted as

something to be avoided. It is relatively easy and cost-effective to install a mini treatment plant to extract the nitrates and other pollutants. To reduce running costs, it may be preferable for the treated water for drinking to be on a separate service from the taps that are used for wash down purposes. Water treatment is not, as yet, considered essential but its future use is likely to depend on the quality of water from the mains supply.

Some estates have the benefit of their own water supply. The value of this asset should not be underestimated. Many people have, in the past, seen the well or bore hole as a burden with its upkeep and maintenance costs, but the benefits of wholesome water are now being appreciated. When the cost of water rises sharply, as in recent years in

The manger insert can be polypropalene, as shown, or galvanised steel. The example above is installed in a cut off corner of a box but could be installed in a wall-mounted bracket.

the UK, coupled with more frequent periods of drought, the benefit of a private supply of water is overwhelming. The quality of bore hole water is generally far superior to that provided through the mains.

When installing the main water supply pipe in a trench to each building, it is good practice to bed and surround the pipe in sand. This is particularly important where flints are present in the ground composition, as there is evidence that the flow of water in the pipes can draw flints into the wall of the pipe, causing a leak.

Mention has been made in a previous chapter regarding the necessity to design the water points in an open yard or in an American barn within easy reach of all boxes. Generally, the water in a stable yard will be fed direct from the mains, however, it is prudent in a medium size or large

establishment to have some of the taps fed from a low-pressure storage tank in case of mains breakdown.

Drainage

One of the most important design points in a stable is the drainage. This is a well-known source of infection but, with good planning and good management practices, these risks can be minimised. To eliminate standing water which can be a source of disease, it is important to ensure the drainage systems work effectively and, to this end, it is necessary to have even and adequate falls, both in the box and around the yard.

A traditional method of drainage within a box is

herringbone grooves set into the concrete floor. These have not proved to be completely successful and are often clogged by straw stems.

Another traditional system for box drainage is a gully sited in the centre or corner of each box. It is now considered that a drainage gully containing foul water within a box is a potential source of trouble due to ammonia gases making the animal prone to respiratory infection. A variation of this in some old stables is the gully on the outside at the back of the building with the floor falling to the back, and a hole through the wall for the foul water to escape and run to the gully. The gullies themselves often then discharged into an open cesspool. This is no longer acceptable from a hygiene point of view and would certainly not be allowed under the tighter legislation now in force.

There is, however, some advantage in the floor falling to the back of the box in that it does not allow urine to escape through the door on to the apron where it can be trodden into and taken from box to box.

The accepted modern method of drainage is to lay the floor of a box to a fall. A fall of 50 mm (2 in) across an average size box or 75 mm (3 in) in a large foaling box is adequate. When straw bedding is laid over the floor, the underlying falls are evened out and cause no physical distress to the animal standing on a non-level surface.

If concrete is used as the floor material, it should either have a very lightly tamped finish in the direction of the fall or, better still, be surfaced with a brushed finish. This latter finish allows free drainage across the surface and easy washing down, while giving no 'troughs' in the concrete to retain ponding water which could become a source of infection. It also gives the horse's hooves a good surface on which to grip.

To take the foul water away, many American barns have been constructed with a continuous, grated channel drain down the centre of the tractor-way, allowing all the floors of the boxes to fall to the central drain within the building. This form of channel can be used with the invert laid to a fall to ensure no hidden foul water collects. These channel systems have ready-made trash gullies to collect waste, straw and other debris which may have got into the system. The advantage of this system is that it looks very neat, as well as being extremely functional. It is also very hygienic if cleaned and flushed out on a daily basis. The regular washing out of the box also washes down the tractor-way and drains.

The disadvantage with grated drains is that the standard specification bolted gratings need to be regularly lifted to clean the trash boxes and maintain the inverts so that they remain clean and free flowing. This is a chore that can discourage regular cleaning. There are 'lay in' gratings which overcome this problem and these should be used whenever possible.

An alternative position for the channel drain is *immediately* at the stable door threshold of a box. This location helps to eliminate any contaminated liquid flowing out on to the apron or tractor-way and being stepped in and carried from box to box. Should the box fall from back to front, then drainage at the door threshold is an excellent idea.

An alternative, less expensive system of drainage is the standard, open, precast concrete channel as used on public highways. These can be laid to falls to gullies but they do entail the adjacent concrete aprons also being laid to similar falls. The advantage of this system is that they are easy to keep clean and any standing water is immediately visible.

The nature of an equestrian yard means there is likely to be lots of straw bedding and other debris to be cleaned up on a daily basis, some of which will inevitably enter the drainage system. This can lead to frequent blockages and raises the risk of infection. In a stable yard, cleaning and flushing of the drains is very important and should become regular practice whichever drainage system is used.

The drainage systems mentioned above refer to drains immediately around the yard. Whatever form of drainage is specified, it will have to be piped to a disposal system.

FOUL WATER DISPOSAL

The disposal of sewage effluent requires consultation with the authorities. Some authorities are not keen to allow foul water discharge from a stable yard into the mains sewer as the antiseptics used can have a neutralising effect on the processing at the sewage treatment plant. If permission is granted by the authority to discharge into the main sewer system, then this is the most convenient and practical solution. On isolated stable establishments consideration should still be given to discharging into the main system if one is available even if it is only made possible by using a small pumping unit.

Where permission is not granted then an on-site disposal system will be required. This will usually mean the construction of a septic tank or cesspool. The former system allows the sediment to settle and break down, with the cleaner liquid being allowed to drain off through a land drainage system into the ground. The cesspool is a water-tight tank which holds all the foul water from the system and so is likely to fill up and require emptying on a more regular basis.

With the privatisation of the water authorities and National Rivers Authority in the UK, rules relating to the discharge of effluent have changed considerably. The NRA may insist that stable effluent either discharges into a cesspool or a silage tank so great care in the design and construction of the drainage system is called for, as unwanted storm water discharging into the cesspool/silage tank will lead to excessive emptying of the tanks, resulting in high running costs.

All effluent from the stable box, including the apron outside the box, must be considered as foul effluent and discharge to the foul sewer system. The general surrounding hard areas within the yard should be considered as surface water areas and the water taken to independent disposal systems so that no storm water discharges into the foul system.

The foul water from the boxes should be arranged so that all drains are easily accessible and an access chamber constructed immediately prior to any disposal system, whether it be a cesspool, septic tank or the main sewer. If a cesspool or septic tank is specified then it needs to be located a minimum of 15 m (17 yd) from any building but close to a road so that access for emptying is convenient. Usually the effluent will be sucked out and taken away by tanker by the local waste disposal company.

The rules for discharge of foul effluent from a dwelling differ from those for equine buildings. A dwelling's foul effluent may discharge to a main sewer, septic tank, cesspool or a modern small treatment plant.

If a main sewer discharge point is not available then the most acceptable of the alternative methods is the self-contained mini treatment works, suitable for small and medium developments including a single house. A mini treatment unit usually requires a 13 amp electrical supply to power a motor which, in turn, rotates the effluent and speeds up the degrading process. The liquid that emanates from the treated sewage is accepted, subject to NRA approval, as suitable for discharge into a water course or a soakaway.

Should a treatment plant or a septic tank require an outfall to a soakaway, then the suitability of the ground should first be checked. Before soakaways are designed, a test should be carried out to ascertain the permeability of the ground. There is a British Standard percolation test (BS6297:1973) which sets out the method for establishing the ability of the land to absorb liquids and determine the amount of soakaway area required on that particular site.

The test, which should be carried out a minimum of three times, involves digging a 300 sq mm (12 sq in) hole 250 mm (10 in) below the invert level. The hole is then filled 250 mm (10 in) deep with water and left overnight. The next day the hole is again filled 250mm (10 in) deep with water and the time it takes for all the water to disappear is recorded.

The formula for determining the requirements is:

The time taken in seconds = Vt
The number of people served by the facility = P
The area of the amount of land drainage required = At
At = P x Vt x 0.25

Electricity

Mention has been made in the previous chapter of various space-heating units, however, this is only part of the total electrical load required for a building.

Apart from the obvious lighting and power point loads, there could be electricity required in the stable yard for specific larger items of equipment such as linseed boilers or oat crushers in the feed store or a feed mill.

Generally, a single-phase electrical supply of 15 kVA is sufficient for a 20-box barn; but requirements concerning specific equipment and also the intention regarding possible future extensions or development need to be considered. The electrical loading and type of equipment will have a direct bearing on whether the supply is single- or three-phase.

The electrical installation for equestrian use will need to be covered by RCB safety cut-out devices and if all buildings on a site are supplied through one meter, then secondary submeters will need to be installed for any dwellings as these are subject to different VAT regulations.

The wiring of the installation should be in conduit for safety and all fittings on the circuits will need to be of moisture-proof type. Many moisture-proof fittings are available. It is now possible to specify a weatherproof socket which will take a standard domestic plug and still remain waterproof.

A range of moisture-proof wall switches is also available and should be specified for all positions in the stable yard installation.

Heating

The horse is naturally equipped to cope with the elements. Its coat thickens or sheds in response to temperature and seasons. Many horse owners believe that horses and foals left out in their paddocks in all but the severest weather actually become hardened and, accordingly, develop into sounder animals. In many instances the requirement to protect and keep the animal warm is solely by the use of a rug or blanket. The horse does not require artificial heating to keep it warm but certain aspects require consideration.

When the animal is clipped, nature has been interfered with. Like humans, horses can catch a cold or other infections and it is normal to provide some boxes with the facility to warm the animal especially if it is sick. This is usually done by the installation of infra-red heaters in the box. These can be turned on or off individually according to the animal's need and their efficiency is based on the fact that an infra-red light replaces body heat but does not heat the surrounding air.

These heaters can be switched on for a short period when the horse returns from exercise in order to dry its coat gently. Alternatively, the heaters can be used for effective treatment of such ailments as pulled muscles or to keep a sick animal warm.

Example of an infra-red heater suitable for warming an animal or person without wasting energy on heating the surrounding air. Ideal for the crush, foaling units or for sick animals.

For foaling boxes, higher output infra-red heaters can be installed. These lights have the facility to be partly turned on should the full power not be required.

Heating should certainly be provided in a sick box or utility box and also in the crush.

Heating for other general rooms, such as the tack room, blanket room, sitting up room, office and mess room, should be considered. All require heat for different purposes. The tack room requires steady background heat while the blanket room requires increased levels of heat to dry out damp rugs. The office and mess room require heat for the comfort of the occupants during the day, while the sitting up room requires heat output at night. It is essential that where a high level of heat is put into a space then that space should be well insulated.

One of the most effective heaters for the tack room is an electric tube heater which can be fixed at low level to provide gentle heat to the tack stored higher up.

A type of heating unit which should be considered for the sitting up room is the electrical combi-heater. This provides heat from a storage heater which takes cheap overnight electricity but it also has a second switch that gives instant convected heat should the room become cold or the storage heater lose its heat prematurely.

The office needs to be insulated and heated in a manner very similar to that of a domestic dwelling. If it can be linked to a boiler system then this is ideal but in most cases the remoteness of the building may mean that an alternative, such as storage heaters, might need to be considered.

Fire precautions

Fire-detection systems are often installed on larger stable yards when being constructed, on the basis that the development is new and it is an economical time to install a system. Clearly, the value of an animal, both in monetary and emotional terms, is of concern to an owner and this may well influence the decision on whether to install a detection system, as will factors such as the proximity of other stable buildings.

Generally speaking, if the materials used to construct a stable are concrete, block work or other non-combustible materials, the most combustible material will be the bedding. In stables constructed from masonry the risk of fire spreading to the whole yard is reduced, although the fire must be attended to and the animals released immediately for their safety. Where the stables have been constructed from timber, then the whole development is combustible and rapid spread of fire through the yard needs to be considered.

In all yards there will be a water standpipe and this can be used initially for tackling a fire. Should the yard house 20 animals or more then consideration should be given to provision of a fixed hose reel extinguisher located in a central ancillary room, such as the feed store, with a hose long enough to reach the extremes of the yard.

When designing plumbing or designing the routes for pipework, it is important that the supply into the building is taken initially to the hose reel should one be installed, and that the pipework is of adequate diameter to supply sufficient pressure.

Whether or not an alarm system is installed, it is essential to install an array of water/gas extinguishers strategically spaced around the yard and in each of the buildings.

Dry powder or CO_2 extinguishers should be installed in all buildings where electrical equipment is used, such as the feed store, tack room and implement shed.

In the UK, it is not usual to install a fire fighting/sprinkler system, possibly due to the good fortune that there has been no major loss of animals caused by fire destroying a building. In the USA, where there have been major losses of buildings and horses through fire, sprinkler systems are considered a necessity.

When alarm systems are installed they frequently give rise to false alerts, often due to the presence of dust particles in the air and this is one reason why alarm systems are not more commonly installed.

The question of whether a fire alarm system or sprinkler system is required is one that only the owner can provide the answer to.

In a traditional yard the construction does give the opportunity to continue the party/division walls between the boxes up to the roof and this effectively constructs a fire break in the roof space to stop the spread of fire. If, however, the box roof/division walls are left open, then, as a minimum fire precaution, the division walls should be taken to the roof of every fourth box to restrict a major spread of fire in case of an outbreak.

Subdivision cannot be so easily achieved in an American barn and therefore greater consideration should be given to an alarm system. The type of system chosen should be considered carefully. The alarm systems most frequently used in barns are detector beams which are less susceptible to being set off by dust than smoke or heat detectors. In every case, it is important that the actual siren/bell is located outside the building, possibly on a gable end and closest to the part of the building to where people are most likely to be alerted by the activated siren.

CCTV

Closed circuit television is widely used on stables both for security and for observing the animals.

For security, it is a visual method of control with cameras positioned to overlook key points, e.g. entrances, tack room and/or individual boxes.

It is usual for the cameras to be linked to monitors by coaxial cable and this is best installed in underground ducts, giving the facility to change or upgrade in the future with minimal disruption and cost. This is particularly important with the rapid advancement and improvement of technology.

The use of CCTV for observing the animals mainly occurs on stud farms to keep a continuous check on the progress of a mare about to drop her foal. A camera is usually set up in each foaling box, linked to a controller, with monitors located in the manager's, and possibly also in the stud groom's, house. There may also be a monitor in the sitting up room adjacent to the foaling boxes.

The controller can be set to switch from box to box so that the viewer can observe the progress of each mare at regular intervals. The controller can be programmed for a predetermined period of time before switching to the next box in sequence.

Modern electronics also enable a split screen allowing all the boxes to be displayed on the screen at the same time. The facility of sound is also useful on a stud farm as this can be an accurate indicator to alert the observer when a mare's waters break or, indeed, to a potential problem when foaling.

Security systems using CCTV can be provided for the whole stables to try to detect unwanted intruders or for supervision of individual boxes.

The tack room is often the area most prone to unauthorised entry. An infra-red detector with an obvious siren out of reach is highly desirable as is a sign indicating that the room has an alarm system. Physical precautions should also be taken and these are mentioned in the text on tack rooms (see page 33).

Chapter Six

Construction and materials

Over many years traditional construction and materials have been used in the building of stables and these have proved to be satisfactory.

Walls

Most stables are constructed with walls of brickwork, blockwork or timber. The differential movement between brickwork and blockwork requires that this movement is taken up by 'designed in' movement joints in order to avoid cracking. Generally, a movement joint is not required on the front of a traditional yard as the front wall is broken up into small lengths of wall by the stable doors. On the rear of the boxes, where the continuous lengths of walling are considerably greater, movement joints are needed approximately every two to four boxes. With sensible planning of the downpipe positions, it is usually possible to hide the joints from general view.

The same criterion regarding movement joints applies equally to the manure bunker. Many manure bunkers are found to be cracked and this is usually due to the bunker being regarded as a purely utilitarian structure. However, to the visitor it promotes the image of a poorly managed and maintained establishment.

When deciding on the material for the wall of the stable, the weight and strength of a horse must be taken into consideration. The most commonly used material for the inside walling of a box is dense blockwork which has proved to be strong and durable. At vulnerable positions in the wall, such as at door or window openings and below grilles or where the blockwork is not otherwise adequately restrained, it may be necessary to introduce horizontal joint reinforcement to withstand the thrusts made by the horse against it.

At door jambs and window jambs, most manufacturers produce what is known as a standard special bullnose block and these have the advantage that there is then no arris on which the horse can damage itself. Apart from the physical benefit of having rounded corners so that injury is less likely, it is also possible to omit door rollers and save their cost.

Although not a necessity, it is good practice to introduce insulation in new wall construction. It is a relatively inexpensive material and can be a great help in minimising the risk of condensation, significantly helping the air quality in the stable.

Stable doors

The box door receives heavy use, particularly the bottom door. Stable doors are, by necessity, wide and heavy and need to be strong enough to withstand kicking by the horse. A standard box door and frame from one of the equine joinery suppliers can be used. These vary from a basic door up to a hardwood door complete with galvanised inner anti-kick sheet. All timber doors require an anti-chew strip on the top edge as do any arrises exposed on the timber frame. Many suppliers also provide mesh or anti-weave grilles as standard units to fit their doors or, indeed, 'made to measure' sizes if required.

The width of the door needs to be a minimum of 1.1 m ($3\frac{1}{2}$ ft) and may be increased up to 1.5 m (5 ft) for foaling boxes. The greater the width of the door, the greater the problem of sagging or twisting on its hinges. Narrower and cheaper standard doors may be purely ledged and braced but for wider doors it is essential to have them framed to increase the rigidity so that they are more likely to stand up to the rigours of the weather and far less likely to sag in use. Timber stable doors are a constant source of maintenance in most stable yards due to shrinkage and swelling following changes in weather conditions. There are also frequent hinge problems, often as a result of decaying timber at the foot of the frame.

Robust hinges are necessary and, to secure adequate fixings, the frame to receive the door should be substantial and made of a dense timber such as European redwood. Many of today's cheaper softwoods, such as deal, are exceedingly soft and pithy and unable to sustain a good fixing over a period of time. For long-term durability the frame should be set 12 mm ($\frac{1}{2}$ in) above floor level in order to reduce the risk of the timber frame absorbing water from the cleaning of the stables and then rotting.

It is surprising that these continuing maintenance problems with doors and frames have not been more widely addressed in the past. Metal-framed timber stable doors are available which with the use of metal hinges on metal outer frames, completely resolve the problems mentioned above.

Another modern material that totally overcomes maintenance problems is fibreglass. Fibreglass doors with foamed cores are available and can be made to look identical to an ordinary timber stable door, but are so strong that anti-chew, anti-kick and other additions to make a timber door more durable become unnecessary. Additionally, the doors need no decoration, no maintenance, will not rot and can be hung on ordinary heavy-duty door hinges as there is no timber to warp or sag. Finally, and of great appeal, is the fact that the annual task of easing 'sticking' timber doors is avoided. Needless to say, at the moment these doors are more expensive to purchase.

Where possible, the stable door should be hinged on the left-hand side so that a person leading a horse will have their left hand free to open the door, leaving their right hand to control the animal.

Larger doors

The large doors required at the ends of the tractor-way in an American barn or to the feed store or exercise barn create other problems due to their size. If timber is to be used, it is better to frame the doors in laminated timber as this is less susceptible to movement and, size for size, is much stronger than ordinary timber. Care should be taken with the face boarding as thin boarding is subject to 'cupping' or ' blowing' through the effects of sun and rain. The thickness of the board should be a minimum of 16 mm ($^5/_8$ in) finished. The board widths, however, should be kept relatively narrow to minimise shrinkage of the timber in summer. Unsightly shrinkage gaps in dark-stained timber, particularly on the south side of a building, are a continual maintenance problem.

Timber doors or boarding which has been finished with a dark brown or black stain greatly increase the risk of maintenance. The dark surface absorbs more of the sun's rays, causing greater heat build up in the material, resulting in increased shrinkage and consequential material breakdown. If staining is required, then consideration should be given to a lighter-coloured stain if longer-term durability is to be achieved.

On larger doors such as tractor-way doors, consideration should be given to the use of metal-framed doors on rollers. This type of construction is lighter in weight than timber and far less prone to maintenance problems.

Windows

Windows provide an important function in the performance of the stable. Apart from the daylight they allow in, they can also be instrumental in promoting air movement/ventilation within the box.

A typical horizontal sliding window, so often used in stables, can be adjusted to provide just a slit for ventilation or can be slid back completely allowing half ventilation. All ventilation with this type of window is straight into the box and if the window is set at a height for the animal to look out, then the air will be directly on to the animal. On a very windy day this could result in stiff muscles and other problems that are undesirable for the horse's well-being.

An alternative and much preferred window profile is the

louvred light. This has the advantage of directing the wind up into the box and enhances the air flow. A further advantage is that on completely still, windless days, when the only air movement in the box is that created by the stack effect of the heat from the animal, the result of heat rising from the horse tends to draw in fresh air from outside the box as the warm air rises past the louvres.

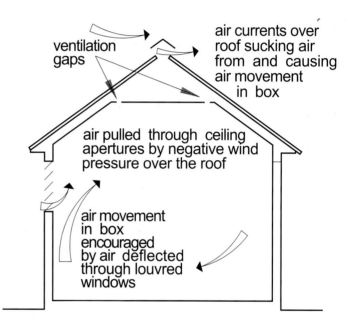

Diagram of air movement in box and louvred window effect.

Louvred windows are by far the best solution, but an alternative that still helps to promote upward air movement in the box is the Sheringham window. The top section of a Sheringham window is hinged to open into the stable and this acts as a deflector, protecting the horse from draughts and pushing the air upward in a very similar way to a conventional louvred window.

Whatever type of window is used, it is essential that the glass is safety glass with a preference for laminated glass rather than toughened glass. All windows should be

61

The grille needs to be sturdy and well secured to the wall or window frame.

protected by strong, galvanised metal grilles internally, with strong vertical bars able to withstand misuse, such as a horse being tied to them instead of to the proper tie ring.

Roof

The roof pitch is a significant factor in the ventilation within a barn or box. A steeper roof pitch (35 degrees minimum) forms a good resistance to wind currents and helps to promote ventilation from the box. A combination of roof pitch, long roof slopes and good

ridge ventilators can help the wind passing over the ridge to create vortices that suck out some of the air from the box or barn, increasing air movement within the box while not creating draughts.

Soffite ventilators can also have their performance enhanced by constructing a reasonable width soffite of, say, 500 mm (20 in). A larger soffite overhang creates a resistance to the wind hitting the wall of the building and the wind is deflected up into the soffite vents, increasing the ventilation rates within the building.

The shape of the roof/ceiling construction can also be used to enhance the flow of air movement within the box. A ceiling that is angled or sloping will avoid corners which encourage stagnant air.

With traditional-type boxes, it is preferable to have a minimum roof pitch of 30 degrees although the pitch may have to increase depending on the type of tile/slate used.

A roof pitch of 35 degrees and above not only helps in the ventilation of a traditional stable, it also helps very significantly in the air movement within an American barn. The wide span of a barn, coupled with a suitable roof pitch, will ensure a large internal air volume to dilute air contaminants and dramatically reduce the chances of condensation. By contrast a roof pitch in the order of 10 degrees will result in an internal space that appears low and claustrophobic with a low air volume. The space inside will become prone to condensation, causing environmental conditions adversely affecting the respiratory performance of the animal.

Although it would not normally be considered sensible to install insulation in an unheated space, it is required in a stable. Insulation above the ceiling keeps the ceiling surface temperature warm and therefore greatly reduces the risk of condensation. The thickness of insulation is of less importance than the fact that some is installed. Even 25 mm (1 in) of insulation will dramatically reduce the likelihood of condensation.

Internal finishes

This is one area where careful detailing can result in money being saved. The box is the animal's home. It must be kept clean and, for the walls, floors and ceiling, this means the ability to withstand regular steam cleaning.

For ceilings, it has been common practice to use exterior quality plywood. However, recent development of materials has led to products which are rot proof, easy to work, have good light reflection and are able to be regularly steam cleaned without any detrimental effect.

Added to these benefits, they also require no decoration. While mentioning decoration, it is important that if this is necessary for a ceiling, then it is best carried out using a matt or satin finish as a high gloss finish is much more likely to give rise to problems with condensation.

The stable walls are often constructed in concrete blockwork finished internally with a render coat of sand and cement. The render coat is no more than a means of providing a smooth surface free from crevices, which can be regularly and hygienically cleaned. In reality, this render coat is a waste of time and money.

Render is a wet process which must dry out before the painting process can be started. It is therefore time consuming as well as costly. With modern, dense concrete blocks, there should be no open pores in the block face which could harbour germs and bacteria. A sensible solution is to have the blockwork walls finished neatly (fairfaced) ready for painting.

Another disadvantage of a render finish in the box is the damage that can be caused by an animal that 'hoof scrapes'. If this happens then the render is left with open pores which can retain bacteria. It also looks unsightly and gives the impression of a poorly maintained yard – the wrong impression to give to a visitor, commercial or otherwise.

With the use of an appropriate paint, a long-lasting, thoroughly durable finish can be applied quickly and economically. Paints such as acrylated rubber have tremendous blocking qualities which fill any crevices or microscopic holes in the blockwork and provide a superbly waterproof finish able to withstand repeated steam cleaning while retaining the quality of the finish. Even with the rough use associated with a stable, the period between recoating can be extended, making it a very cost-effective solution.

Consideration should also be given to an acrylated

rubber painted surface above a dado line, with a boarded material at low level such as timber, plywood or stockboard.

Stockboard is an extremely dense, rot-proof board which can be screwed or stuck to the blockwork. All joints can be sealed and it provides a permanent, maintenance-free finish. Stockboard can also be secured to the wall with horizontal battens that, in themselves, act as casting rails.

Another solution is ribbed rubber sheet which acts as both a durable resilient lining and anti-cast facility. Again, it does away with the expense of render and the delay associated with a wet trade.

A further alternative to those mentioned above is the application of resilient rubber bricks/tiles similar to those used on box floors.

Although not strictly part of the wall finish, casting rails may be required on the box walls. The casting rail height can vary enormously and, sometimes, more than one rail will be necessary. The casting rail has traditionally been made from a very dense timber, such as American oak, due to its ability to withstand biting and the stable environment. Another suitable and particularly neat solution is dense rubber segmental profiles as used by ships chandlers. These rubber profiles are available in various widths, are long lasting, with no maintenance, and provide an ideal grip for the animal. In addition they give a particularly smart appearance when installed.

Floors

In the design of the box, one of the prime considerations is to reduce the risk of infection. Some boxes in old stables had floors of compacted chalk. Although this is a cheap solution, it tends to retain traces of urine. For a Thoroughbred establishment this type of floor is not recommended other than for barren mares' boxes or weanlings' boxes.

The most common material used for the box floor is a concrete slab, laid to fall to a drainage point at either the front or the back of the box. The slab is usually finished with a light tamping or by a brushed finish. The latter is

Typical drainage from an old box.

Opposite: *Rubber on the box wall provides a resilient surface that is hygienic and maintenance free.*

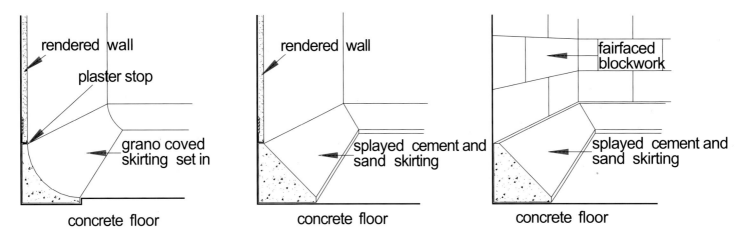

Sketch of coved and splayed skirtings.

most effective, as brushing reduces the likelihood of 'plastic cracking' (fine open pores where bacteria could be retained) in the concrete. Plastic cracking is of no significance to the structural ability but it is important in a box where the cracks can harbour and encourage bacteria.

For riding stables or similar establishments a brushed finish to the concrete areas is useful as it is the easiest surface to keep clean and labour can be kept to a minimum.

When the animal is mainly boxed and does not have the opportunity to spend some time in a resilient grass paddock, it is more important to specify a softer floor surface than concrete. Resilient floors are, however very beneficial to all horses and particularly those which suffer leg problems, as the 'bounciness' of the floor is gentler on the leg joints.

Bedding alone does not provide resilience and comfort to the joints; a horse must have sound legs and joints at all times. Good specification of the flooring can help to achieve this. Common materials are sheet rubber with sealed joints and proprietary rubber compound floors which can be trowelled on.

Also on the market is a resilient rubber brick which can be loose laid or stuck to the concrete floor. This material/product originates from the USA and is little different from the rubber safety surface that is now compulsory below children's play equipment.

Whatever construction or system is used, the floor chosen must be able to be readily and thoroughly cleaned and allow muck and urine to be easily removed and ammonia gases to be neutralised.

It is important to note the benefit of some form of skirting. It is inevitable that, without a skirting, there will be a physical crack around the perimeter of the box between the wall and floor which can be a potential source of infection. Some boxes have been specified with coved skirtings. This is the optimum solution as it is very easy to keep clean and eliminates the presence of arrises. A less expensive alternative is the splayed skirting shown in the diagram above. This is very easy and cheap to construct with semi skilled labour and achieves all the requirements of ease of cleaning and no ponding.

Opposite: Older and well-used boxes can be improved by refurbishment.

External materials

The external materials for the buildings will be chosen with appearance being the main factor, bearing in mind the context in which the building is sited.

Undoubtedly, the planning officer will express an opinion and frequently there will be a request to maintain the local vernacular. Where timber external cladding is called for, there should be a preference for a lighter wood stain for the reasons given previously and below. Brick, stone, blockwork and render are all viable alternative external walls finishes.

Many traditional yards were clad in creosoted boarding. For a new building intended to harmonise with the existing buildings on a site, planed timber, tongued and grooved boarding is often specified. This is then stained in a dark, proprietary stain protective coating to match the existing buildings.

However, after only a year or two, the boarding on the south and west sides of a building often deteriorates significantly. This is caused by the dark colour of the stain absorbing the sun's rays, shrinking the timber and exposing primed-only surfaces. There is also a visible breakdown in the colour of the stain. The deterioration is very pronounced when comparison is made with the east and north sides of a building. Although the sun is the main cause, the problem actually stems from the timber. Today timber is grown more rapidly and therefore has wider, softer, growth bands. Additionally, it is also subjected to kiln drying which leaves the timber less durable than traditional slow, air-dried timber.

This particular problem can be tackled in several ways. Firstly, a lighter stain should be specified as it will help to reduce solar heat gain. Secondly, consideration should be given to specifying shiplap boarding instead of tongue and grooved. The shape of shiplap board has been shown to conceal shrinkage more than tongue and grooved, which highlights the problem. Finally, if and when shrinkage does occur with shiplap, the barer wood is sheltered by the board above, while with tongue and grooved, the bare timber is exposed and creates a potential rot problem.

For the external roof finish, the preference from an aesthetic point of view is natural clay tile or slate. However, alternative look-alike substitutes are available for both products if cost is of particular importance. Even cheaper roofing products are also available, such as profiled sheet, when cost is paramount.

Exterior yard surface materials

The exterior ground surface material provides a large part of the visual attraction of a yard. Concrete, although durable and a satisfactory surface material, is unsightly in large areas, although it can be topped with hot tar and surface shingle dressing to improve the appearance. However, the non-resilient nature of concrete will mean that the applied surface dressing does not bind down integrally with the concrete and some surface separation will occur, particularly on corners where vehicle wheel movement is frequent.

A new product is now available that overcomes this debonding. It is based on polyurethane and allows almost any surface dressing to be used.

Asphalt is a popular surface material in stable yards. Although this is marginally more attractive than plain concrete, it is still a rigid material.

Macadam is another frequently used material which has a surface that offers more resilience than concrete or asphalt and will give a good grip for the animals. However, it can become slippery in slightly damp and frosty conditions. It is widely available in many different colours and, where appearance is of importance, is a good choice.

Opposite: *Selected shingle is a common external surfacing material along with macadam or brick paviors.*

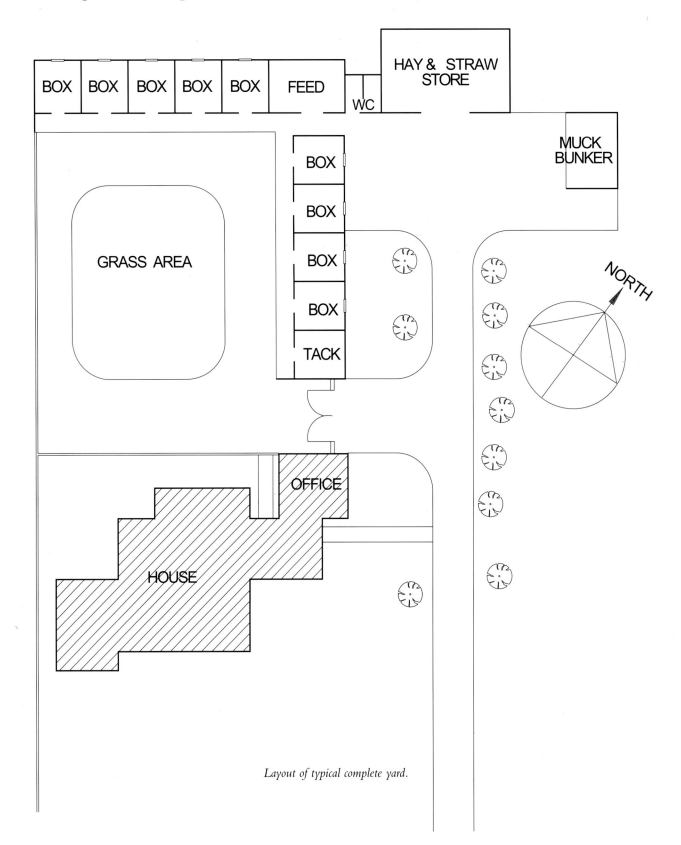

Layout of typical complete yard.

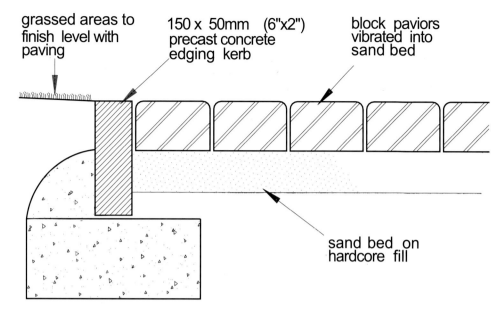

grassed areas to finish level with paving

150 x 50mm (6"x2") precast concrete edging kerb

block paviors vibrated into sand bed

sand bed on hardcore fill

Typical concrete block paving detail.

For many yards a popular material is concrete block paviors. These have reduced dramatically in price and can provide a most attractive finish which is non-slip and easy to clean and large areas can be laid very quickly. In addition, the block laying provides a construction to enable repairs which are virtually invisible, unlike concrete or macadam.

For external hard areas such as roadways and access ways, which are visible from the public highway, the local authority may prefer materials with finishes other than concrete or asphalt, both of which are harsh to the eye. On equine establishments in rural environments a suitable finish is sprayed-on shingle which can be very attractive but does give the estate a regular maintenance task.

For a service yard which is generally not on view to the public, concrete provides the best surface. This is easy to keep clean and is better able to withstand the heavy loads associated with bulk feed and bedding deliveries and the wear from vehicles turning.

As mentioned in the first paragraph on exterior yard surface materials, the roadways provide a large part of the visual attraction of a development. Part of this visual attraction is the verge area beside the roadway, which is frequently put down to grass. It is good practice, when regrading the areas beside the road at the end of a project, to sow the verges with a slow-growing grass seed which cuts down on future maintenance but still provides an attractive appearance.

71

Chapter Seven
Basic/DIY stables

This chapter considers basic stables for an owner with only one or a few animals and for those owners wishing to provide DIY stable accommodation. Before embarking on a DIY project, make a realistic assessment of your practical skills. If you decide that, in the long term, it might be cheaper (and certainly considerably quicker) to employ a local builder to construct the stable, the following points will still assist in establishing exactly what type of construction is required.

The principal requirements for a stable are as already discussed in the introduction. The three ways to achieve basic stable accommodation are:

- prefabricated
- traditional masonry
- timber framed.

When making a decision on the type of stabling, whether prefabricated timber or masonry construction, it is prudent to consider the maintenance and durability of the box. If a short-term, low-cost building is required, then timber prefabricated boxes may be the best solution.

If, however, the intention is to make a longer-term investment, then more substantial boxes should be considered.

Will the stable require planning permission? This will depend on the location and size of the building. A single stable or even a double stable is likely to be below the size of 70 cu m (92 cu yd) that requires planning consent in the UK.

If the stable to be erected is within the grounds of a listed building or in a conservation area, then it almost certainly will require Listed Building Consent which is separate from, and should not be confused with, planning permission.

An informal approach to the planning authority at an early stage, to confirm the requirement for a planning application, is always to be recommended.

Prefabricated stables

For the small establishment possibly the most economical way to construct a stable yard is to purchase 'off the peg' timber prefabricated units. These are readily available from many specialist suppliers. Timber prefabricated boxes also offer a good solution where stables are required quickly.

When considering this type of box, it is important to make comparisons among the various types and, if possible, visit a stable yard where the make you have tentatively selected has been in use for some time, to establish how well it stands up to the rigours of use.

Check out the comparative sizes of boxes and what each specification contains. Check whether the package includes basic necessities such as an anti-chew strip or toughened glass or whether these items are optional extras.

Give full consideration to the quality of materials and workmanship used by each manufacturer, rather than making a decision solely on cost. The prefabricated stable yard that has stood up well to ten years' use will still be of some value, while possibly cheaper, inferior boxes that have become careworn will detract from the appearance of the premises and be of no value. Even more serious, dilapidated boxes could be a danger to the animals' safety or be a breeding ground for infection and vermin.

The manufacturer's quoted price for a prefabricated box will generally be for the superstructure only. Check whether the price includes erection.

Over and above the cost of the prefabricated shell are the costs incurred with the local builder for foundations, floor bases, drainage, electrical installation, plumbing and external works, all necessary to make the shell usable.

One of the most important factors is the siting. Once built, the boxes will be expensive to move elsewhere. Minor alterations to a building can take place relatively cheaply, but relocation is expensive. Make sure you are satisfied with the siting and that all factors have been considered, including prevailing winds, aspect, access, services and ground conditions. Consideration must also be given to the proximity of other buildings, trees and the effect of orientation.

Some stables have front window vents beside the stable door as standard, while others have windows at the rear. The preference should always be for windows and vents at the rear so that there is a good flow of air *across* the box.

Timber prefabricated boxes are unsuitable for ponies or horses that are going to spend most of their day in the box. As with any timber shed construction, timber boxes become uncomfortably hot in summer and uncomfortably cold in winter. Historically, advice from equine experts has suggested that the horse should be stabled in conditions that are in the 50-60 °F (10-15 °C) range for comfort and to reduce the risk of infection. This cannot be achieved with lightweight timber construction.

The open-textured nature of timber leaves it more prone to hiding bacterial spores, while the softness of the material means that it has to be protected by an anti-chew strip in order to avoid being damaged by crib biting.

For situations where the animal is in its box for large parts of the day, therefore, traditional masonry built boxes are preferable.

DIY stables

PLANS AND PERMISSIONS

The first task is to draw a sketch of the building. Include notes on the materials to be used, taking care to create a stable complementing both the adjacent buildings and the environment. If necessary, go to the local builders merchants where a large range of materials will be on display from which the choice can be made.

After the drawing has been finished and the relevant permissions obtained, it is necessary to tackle the practicalities of building.

SIZE

The size of the box will depend on the size of the animal to be housed. A stable box 3 x 3 m (10 x 10 ft) with a ceiling height of 2.3 m (7 ft) will be adequate for a Shetland pony.

A larger horse will require a larger box up to about 4.5 x 4.5 m (15 x 15 ft) for a broodmare, allowing her to move around freely and with a ceiling height of 3.5m (11.5 ft). Boxes for special purposes, such as foaling boxes, will need to be even larger.

FOUNDATIONS AND SLAB

A preliminary check on the ground conditions should be made to determine the width and depth of foundation required. For economy and ease of construction, where good ground conditions exist, the concrete floor may be thickened out at the edges in lieu of individual wall strip foundations. However, these thickened out concrete edges also need to be reinforced and tied into the slab reinforcement.

To prevent movement and cracking of the super-

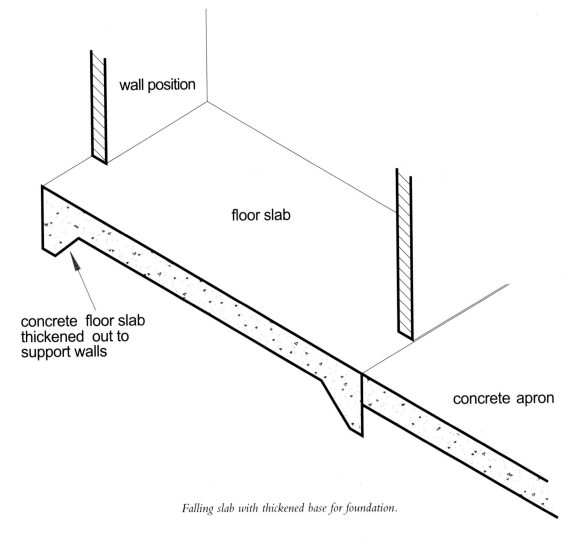

wall position

floor slab

concrete floor slab
thickened out to
support walls

concrete apron

Falling slab with thickened base for foundation.

Simple masonry pony boxes.

structure, the floor slab should be reinforced with mesh reinforcement. The concrete floor slab itself should be a strong mix (1:2:4, C25) and laid to a minimum depth of 125 mm (5 in). The slab should be laid with a 50 mm (2 in) cross fall to allow natural drainage of the urine out of the box and to enable the box to be washed down. A cross fall will eliminate puddles of standing water or urine and reduce the risk of spreading infection.

The concrete floor slab should be finished with a light tamping in the direction of the fall or with a brushed finish to provide a good grip for the horse's hoofs, while allowing liquid to drain away.

While the concrete floor slab is still wet, provision should be made for any fixings that are required to secure the walls to the concrete base. It is much easier to provide fixing points while the concrete is still wet than to have to drill the concrete when it has set.

MASONRY BOXES

If the box walls are constructed from blockwork, then a lightweight pony could be contained within 100 mm (4 in) dense concrete block walls while a medium-

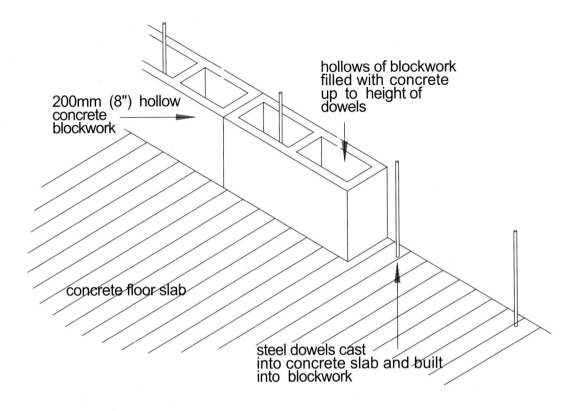

200mm (8") hollow concrete blockwork

hollows of blockwork filled with concrete up to height of dowels

concrete floor slab

steel dowels cast into concrete slab and built into blockwork

Diagram of floor dowels.

weight pony or horse should have a minimum of 150 mm (6 in) dense concrete blockwork. For heavy horses a 225 mm (9 in) block wall will be required.

Whichever thickness of blockwork is used, the wall can be strengthened still further by laying reinforcement mesh in the mortar joints. Brickwork reinforcement, if used, should be continued up to the height of the animal's withers.

If blockwork is used for the walls, and particularly if 100 mm (4 in) dense blocks or 200 mm (8 in) hollow blocks are used, they will need to be secured to the concrete base with mild steel dowels cast into the concrete and built into the blockwork. This will prevent the possibility of lateral movement of the walls should the animal kick out or lean against the wall.

TIMBER-BUILT BOXES

Much the same floor base is required as mentioned on pages 74 and 75, however, provision should be made to secure the timber framing to the concrete slab.

When timber is to be used for the stable walls, it should sit on a course or two of semi-engineering bricks which should be secured to the base with anchor bolts or metal straps.

Certainly, the timber-constructed box should not sit immediately on the slab, otherwise the timber in contact with the slab/ground will quickly become damp and rotten. In addition, it will rapidly become a source for infection. It is essential that a damp course is installed below the timber plate.

The framing for the timber structure must be treated

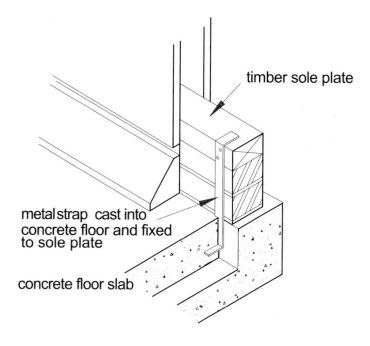

timber sole plate

metal strap cast into
concrete floor and fixed
to sole plate

concrete floor slab

Diagram of floor/wall junction of timber box.

with preservative, as should any of the cladding boards for the external face. The internal surface, at a level up to the horse's withers, should also be lined with a strong smooth sheet material. For economy and strength, sterling board or plywood will provide a safe, cleanable surface and will also add rigidity to the structure. The outside can be clad with sheeting or timber boarding, whichever is appropriate for the site.

ROOFING

The roof for the DIY economy stable is best constructed from corrugated metal or fibre sheeting. Both of these materials can be obtained in a variety of different colour finishes to blend in with the other buildings around the site. Roof sheeting requires support from purlins across the width of the stable and

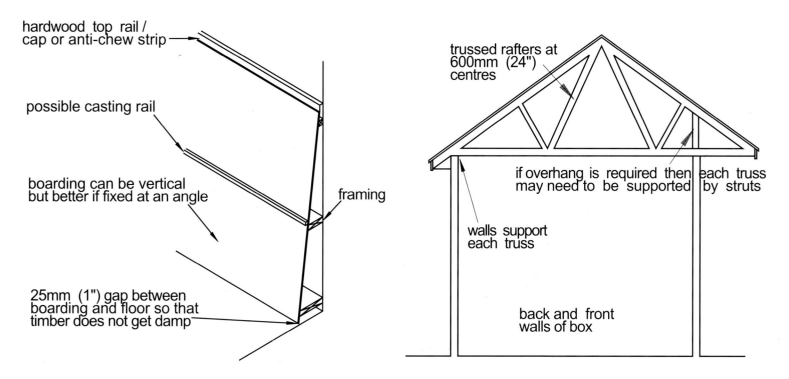

hardwood top rail /
cap or anti-chew strip

possible casting rail

boarding can be vertical
but better if fixed at an angle

framing

25mm (1") gap between
boarding and floor so that
timber does not get damp

Diagram of timber lining to stable.

trussed rafters at
600mm (24")
centres

if overhang is required then each truss
may need to be supported by struts

walls support
each truss

back and front
walls of box

Diagram of roof construction.

these should be supported on the cross walls.

If roof sheeting materials are used, it is essential that they are of twin skin construction with an insulation layer in between to reduce condensation on the inside of the roof sheet making the stable damp.

A key factor in creating adequate ventilation is to have a good volume of air in the box, therefore do not skimp on the height of the box.

Apart from the ventilation providing fresh air for the animal, it also removes damp air from the stable which is, in itself, a potential source of infection.

If a more attractive and traditional appearance is required for the roof, a pitched roof is extremely easy to construct by using prefabricated trussed rafters obtainable from a builders merchant. These trussed rafters will be supplied to the span required and will need to be erected at about 600 mm (24 in) apart and secured to the walls with steel straps. However, once erected they can be felted and tiled or slated with ease and give a long lasting roof with low maintenance.

WINDOWS AND DOORS

Once the main structure has been completed, there remains the easier task of fitting the secondary elements of the stable.

The windows, doors, door frames, grilles and other fittings can all be purchased from an equine joinery supplier and should be well fixed into the openings previously constructed.

Accessory fittings such as rainwater goods can be obtained from the local builders merchant and should be installed in accordance with the manufacturer's instructions.

Once the main envelope of the stable has been completed, there only remains the fitting out.

STABLE FIXTURES AND FITTINGS

Fitting out a stable is, in part, necessary to make management of the animal easier, while it is also a case of personalising the stable to your own particular needs.

There is an abundance of fixtures and fittings that may be installed in a stable to make the job of managing the animal more convenient. The most important elements are the feed manger and the water point.

For horse owners wishing to know the quantity of water the animal is drinking per day, the most common manger is the corner type made of galvanised metal, stainless steel or heavy duty polythene. All of these can be purchased

A typical hay rack fixed in the corner of a box.

from an equine supply merchant. They can be fixed direct to the wall or built into the corner where they utilise otherwise wasted space. The corner mangers can be used for feed or water and can easily be lifted out for daily cleaning.

The alternative to the removable water manger is the auto drinker. These require a plumbed supply into each box as opposed to one supply into a yard/range of boxes, but are labour saving and ensure that a fresh supply of water is available to the animals at all times. Auto drinkers are available as a small bowl type or range up in size from 1-5 litre ($1^{3}/_{4}$–9 pt) tank versions. The larger types are controlled by a ball float and have a deeper trough which stores the water. However, the ball float type on these larger versions tends to be noisier than the centre float type used in the small bowls. Additionally, the deeper trough makes cleaning more difficult.

Auto drinkers are available in enamel finish and galvanised. It is recommended that the enamel be used as these are much easier to clean than galvanised drinkers which tarnish quickly.

Apart from the water and feed manger, other fittings that may be required include:

- salt lick holder
- hay net ring
- tie ring(s)
- door rollers
- casting rails
- door and window grilles.

The location for the hay net tie ring should be away from the water manger and secured at a height where the horse does not have to reach up to it so that dust cannot fall into the animal's eyes and nose.

The tie ring for securing the animal while grooming

etc. is also an important fitting. Tie rings are available with different fixings for both timber and masonry applications. For masonry it is possible to build the tie ring into the wall as the stable is being constructed or to surface fix it to the wall on completion. Surface fixing is less secure than 'through the wall' types. If the stable is constructed with timber walling, then metal plate washers are necessary on either side of the timber in order to make the fixing secure.

The window grille should never be used as a substitute for a tying point. Window grille bars can become bent, or worse, if the grille is pulled off the wall, it could result in serious damage to animal and stable hand.

Door grilles are not essential for every stable but, if required, can be installed simply by a pair of sockets fixed to the back of the bottom door. The grilles can be made to measure or be standard 'off the peg' ones from an equestrian supplier. There are basically two types: the full mesh grille which does not allow the horse to put its head outside the box, and the anti-weave type that allows the animal to put its head outside the box but restricts it from weaving from side to side.

FIELD SHELTER

Where there is a particularly restricted budget and DIY skills are limited, consideration might be given to a field shelter as an alternative to a stable. This will provide shelter for a pony but is really only suitable for occasional use for a hardy animal and should not be considered a longer-term solution or if the animal frequently needs the use of a stable.

Use of old stables

In some situations there may be the opportunity to re-use a stable that has fallen into disuse over the years.

Old stables should be checked for potential dangers to the animal. Carefully inspect the structure to ensure it is still robust and structurally sound and that there are no dangerous projections (loose wire and nails) which could cause injury.

Check the electrical installation. Ensure all wiring is in conduits and the wiring and fittings are out of the reach of the animal. If the light fitting already exists, check that it is not the domestic pendant type. It should be the waterproof external bulkhead type or the waterproof and damage-resistant fluorescent type, preferably with a metal protection guard. The light switch should be located outside the stable and also be of the external waterproof specification.

Thoroughly clean out the stable and spray all surfaces down with stable disinfectant.

Check the floor to ensure there are no uneven parts or depressions where ponding can occur or infectious bacteria be harboured. The floor should have a good fall to remove any urine. If the old floor is inadequate, several products are available which can be used for filling holes or levelling the old floor in order to achieve an even, non-slip, free-draining area.

Check the security of the door and the height of the lower stable door. It is unsatisfactory if the door is too high and the horse cannot see out. The door should have, as a minimum, a sliding bolt catch for security and, preferably, a kick-over latch at the bottom.

Field care

The paddock for the pony or horse must be a place where the animal can be contained in safety.

Before the animal is allowed into any field, it is important to take a very close look at the areas that could give rise to danger.

First look at the paddock fencing. This should be sound and strong, preferably of the two- or three-rail post and rail type or the equestrian fencing mesh type. However, strand wire and post is also adequate on a temporary basis. Check for any barbed wire and remove it together with any loose or jagged ends of wire from previous fencing. Check the posts; these should be firmly bedded into the ground as horses like to rub against firm objects such as posts and any weak points will be sure to be found out and could lead to a possible escape route for the animal.

For the commercial establishment new fencing is best installed by a reputable firm who have experience in this specialist work.

If cheap and temporary fencing is required, then electric tape fencing should be considered. The horse is susceptible to electric shocks and will stay well away from the electric fence after the first few initial shocks. Its keen sense of hearing will also tell it if the electric fencing is active, which it will detect from the electric pulses.

Electric fencing can be installed quickly and is particularly useful in an emergency. It can also be used effectively to rotate areas of paddock that are to be temporarily rested from grazing. Recent improvements in the quality of electric tape and fittings have made it a much more durable fencing solution.

Check the hedging and trees; remove any protruding branches that could injure the horse. After the hedging and fencing have been checked, pay attention to the gate. This should be able to be easily opened by the handler but with a catch or secure fastening mechanism which prevents the inquisitive horse from playfully releasing it. A chain with a spring clip is ideal, as is a hook with a safety clip.

The next item to turn your attention to is the plant life. Check if there are any poisonous trees or weeds within the paddock or within reach of the animal. Remove all yew trees and laburnum trees. Other plants that are poisonous to the horse are ragwort, rhododendron, privet, bryony and deadly nightshade and all should be dug up and burnt. Remember also that the beautiful oak tree sheds its poisonous acorns in the autumn and horses should not be allowed to eat them. Either temporarily fence off the oak tree and remove the acorns in one go or remove the acorns daily from the paddock.

The horse will require access to a permanent supply of clean fresh water. Ideally, this should be in a trough fed by a wholesome supply with the pipes buried underground below frost level. The riser pipe to the trough should be insulated to give it protection from the frost and should be fitted with a turn-off valve to help with maintenance of the trough.

If a main supply to the paddock is not available then a cheap alternative is a plastic bin which can be purchased from most equestrian suppliers.

Finally, before releasing the horse into the paddock, remember that the area most likely to cut up is around the gate. So that poaching of the gateway is not exacerbated, ensure the water trough or butt is placed away from the gate.

One solution to reducing the chances of a quagmire at the gate is to raise this area slightly with rolled in limestone or chalk. The latter, if used, can be consolidated still further by raking half a bag of cement dust into the chalk surface prior to rolling.

In poor weather the horse will stand with its back to the prevailing winds. If there is a tree or hedging the animal will position itself to gain the most protection. To provide additional protection in the paddock the cheapest form is probably the field shelter. These can be purchased from any equine supply merchant and installed without the need for a base. Select a location that gives protection from the prevailing winds yet allows the animal see what is approaching when it is standing in the shelter.

Although field shelters can be made simply, the cost of an 'off the peg' timber unit is not excessive and is preferable to the untidy mismatch of materials which is often the effect of a do-it-yourself exercise and results in an untidy look to the countryside.

The horse will only eat relatively short grass so if much of the pasture has overlong grass, it may be necessary to 'top' the grass (cut it down to a suitable height for grazing).

The number of ponies/horses to the hectare is very much dependent on the quality of grass and breed of animal and size. It may be that four Thoroughbreds to 4 hectares (10 acres) is adequate on good grazing while heavy hunters may require more land per animal. A section D Welsh Mountain pony would be quite content with inferior quality grass and a smaller area.

Chapter Eight

Paddocks, manure bunkers and services

Paddocks

The layout and planning of paddocks should be seen as an integral part of the whole development. At an early stage the design and layout of the whole estate should co-ordinate the various elements including buildings, services, access routes, paddock layouts, planting schemes and contact with the statutory authorities. Ideally, this should also include the provision of new hedges, trees and shelter belts which are all essential to provide the horses with the best possible environment in which to grow and thrive.

The manager/owner will, without doubt, have firm views on how the paddocks are to be laid out, based on the method by which the establishment will be managed. It is recommended that expert advice is taken to co-ordinate and give technical advice on the best method for servicing the estate, i.e. positions for stopcock controls on services, emergency controls, road specification and layout of access roads, etc.

The layout of paddocks is generally determined by proximity to the boxes, topography, location of trees and shelter belts. It is preferable to locate the smaller nursery paddocks close to the boxes with paddocks increasing in size the further they are away from the building.

Wet and muddy paddocks are a source of ailments for the horse in the form of diseases such as mud fever and foot rot. In order to reduce the risk of the paddock becoming churned up, muddy and hence a risk to the horses' health, the siting of water troughs and gates needs to be carefully considered. Horses frequently congregate near the gate and it is therefore preferable not to locate gates of adjacent paddocks directly opposite one another. The same applies to the location of the water trough points.

Should money be available, it is becoming increasingly popular to construct hard standings at the points most vulnerable to overuse. Hard standing at the gate and trough positions can be formed in stone such as ironstone or limestone which should be laid and compacted to finish slightly above the general grass level. The hard standings should then be rolled in smooth. An alternative, cheaper solution is to use well compacted chalk which can be made more durable by raking a bag of cement dust into the surface prior to rolling. Any of the methods mentioned will help to eliminate a potentially boggy area.

It is also advantageous for the gates to be located on an elevated part of the paddock, meanwhile bearing in mind the need to manage the estate efficiently in terms of ease of bringing in the animals when required. Gates in low corners of paddocks are to be avoided as, generally, the low areas are the wettest parts of the field and young foals and yearlings are inclined to 'race' to the corner when being called in. If this area is low and wet, the risk of injury is greatly increased by the possibility of the animals sliding into the fencing.

If paddocks are low lying and generally poorly drained, then, for the benefit of the animals and pasture growth, a land drainage system should be considered. The cheapest and quickest solution is to have the paddock mole drained. However, this is only a short-term solution and may have to be repeated at frequent intervals. A longer-term solution is to have a proper land drainage system installed. This is best carried out by a drainage contractor who will use a special land drainage machine that cuts the ground, installs the drainage pipe, complete with shingle surround, and leaves the field on completion with very little physical damage. The paddock can then be in use very shortly after installation of the drainage system.

There is always room to consider how the well-being of the animal can be improved. The paddock is no exception. Very few paddocks have a tree or copse of trees under which the animals can stand to shelter from the elements. On a hot day how often is the horse seen standing in the shade when given the option to do so? Hedges or trees within paddocks also provide great benefits during cold and windy weather. During inclement weather the horse will use its hindquarters to protect the rest of its body and will back up to a hedge or tree to increase this protection when given the opportunity. These natural instincts show the need to

maintain trees and hedge shelter belts in good condition to provide the best conditions for the well-being of the animal. Hedge and tree shelter belts are also particularly important in protecting young foals from the worst of the weather and it is good practice to create shelter belt hedges in hawthorn or beech or, indeed, a mixture of both. The beech hedge has the advantage that it retains some of its leaves through winter, providing a good shield against the cold winds.

Provision of new shelter belt hedging and tree belts for the protection of the animal is a necessity if they do not already exist on the land to be developed. The cost of trees and hedges can be quite considerable, running into tens of thousands of pounds. With professional advice, it is possible to obtain grants in the UK for a large majority of these costs. Current concerns with regard to the environment mean that grants may be obtained from such organisations as county councils, district councils, MAFF, the Countryside Commission and other similar groups. Time spent on researching all sources of revenue can be very worthwhile, both from the financial grant point of view and the fact that, with grant aid, the owner may well be tempted into providing additional tree belts and hedging, to the greater benefit of the animals.

The general advice from arboriculturalists is to specify hedging and tree shelter belts in species native to the area in which the development is taking place. This makes good sense as the land has proven to be good for those species. It is common practice to mix species and where some trees with slow growth patterns are used, it is preferable to intermix the main species with an occasional quick-growing, non-native tree, such as a conifer, in order to provide some early worthwhile shelter, and to provide some protection to the young native species.

If there is a general lack of shelter on a new and barren site and field shelters cannot be afforded, suitable protection can still be achieved by constructing close or

Yorkshire boarding at the corners of the paddock fences. If all corners are similarly treated then, whatever the direction of the inclement weather, the animals can still obtain some shelter.

PADDOCK FENCING

Paddock fencing is usually carried out as a separate direct order with a specialist fencing contractor and can be either traditional post and rail fencing or the more modern 'keep safe' type fence which is a metal mesh supported by posts and a top rail. The traditional post and rail can be either two-, three- or four-rail with the height determined by the manager's preference and the type and size of the animal to be contained; the normal height being around 1.4 m (4½ ft) for Thoroughbred racehorses. It is usual for stallion paddocks to be fenced to a greater height; in the region of 1.75 m (5½ ft). Should the stallion paddock(s) not be located in isolation, then additional measures may need to be taken, such as close boarding the whole paddock in order to control unwanted behaviour by the stallion.

The advantage often put forward for use of the 'keep safe' type wire fence is that the mesh is small enough to keep out rabbits, foxes, dogs, etc. If this type of fence is not to be generally used for the paddocks, it still has many advantages as a perimeter fence, especially where rights of way exist.

Services and roadways

By necessity, any development will involve the installation of water and electricity services and, if several buildings are involved, will include the construction of access roadways and maybe service ductwork for future installation upgrades.

Careful thought given to the layout route for services

and for pipe diameters, stopcock positions etc., can make the estate more efficient in general and less wasteful should a leak occur.

The route of water services and the location of valves, stopcocks and flushing points can best be planned on the drawing board for optimum efficiency. The emergency stopcocks should be conveniently located for easy access and, following installation, should be surveyed and documented for the client's record purposes. Many valuable minutes can be lost searching for water pipe routes and valves when an emergency has occurred and, in the present day, when water is becoming an expensive commodity, the need for a planned, inspected and recorded layout is all the more important.

On isolated establishments there occasionally exists a private bore hole with a licence to extract water. With advice from a specialist, this facility can be a tremendous asset (see page 51).

Should the site be isolated but still have access to a mains water supply, then consideration should be given to a water storage facility on the estate. This not only overcomes any problems of lack of water in a drought or in times when water pressure is low, it can also act as an emergency source of water in the case of a fire. As an alternative, many remote stud farms utilise the topography of the land to form an artificial pond which can double as a feature as well as an emergency resource. Should a lake or pond be considered, this will require the consent of the National Rivers Authority.

It is wise to establish at an early stage whether there is a land drainage system already installed in the paddocks as this may play a part in deciding the location of a building and will almost certainly play a part in the discharge of storm water from the building. On a site where there is a large difference in ground levels, siting of water troughs may also be dictated by water pressure or lack of it.

85

Opposite: Note the close boarding on each corner of the paddock fencing, offering some protection to the horse whatever the wind direction.

Entrance Design

While discussing the general layout of the establishment, it is worth mentioning the value of an attractive entrance. The first impression a visiting owner or potential customer/client has of the enterprise is the entrance. If the entrance is well designed, attractive and makes the right impact, the value to a commercial establishment can be immeasurable. The first impression is a lasting one and, although somewhat esoteric, can create the atmosphere of a thriving enterprise and one with which the client wishes to be associated. Conversely, an unkempt establishment, whether a true or false reflection of the business, can be interpreted as a less successful enterprise.

The planning authority will almost certainly take a keen interest in the design for the entrance. The style of the entrance should take account of the type of establishment, its importance and the nature of the surrounding countryside.

Manure bunkers

Changing employment trends during the twentieth century have played a part in the move from traditional yards to the American barn format. At one time labour was cheap and, in stables, this work was usually carried out by men. Today many more stable girls are employed and labour has become a more expensive commodity. This has influenced stable design and the activities within the stable, especially where lifting of loads is required. Today the stable barrow is a commonly used piece of equipment and mucking out is a less physical task.

Also in relation to mucking out, greater use is now made of alternative bedding materials such as shredded newsprint, and wood shavings. It should be noted that the Control of Pollution and Environmental Protection Acts designate waste produced from breeding, boarding, stabling or exhibiting of horses as being industrial waste and, as such, it must be disposed of at a licensed tip.

Flies that are attracted to the manure bring irritation and disease to the horse. This occurs more often in the warm, summer months during the prime competition season. To reduce the problem of flies, it is essential that the manure heap is disposed of frequently and, between emptying, the bunker sprayed with insecticide.

Today there is a tendency for the manure bunker to be emptied less frequently than in the past as the cost of waste removal has risen. This has led to larger and larger manure bunkers being required. The manure bunker needs to be accessible for the stable hand on a daily basis while also being accessible to the waste collection vehicle.

If possible, the bunker should be set to the north east of the building, facing north. This will mean that the walls will give some protection from prevailing winds and also a smaller area of the manure will be exposed to the direct rays of the sun. This will reduce the chance of the prevailing winds blowing loose straw around the yard or, indeed, spreading noxious smells.

For a riding school or stud farm the location of the manure bunker is not quite so critical as the horses are generally out of their boxes. However, the well-being of the animal is equally affected if it is bitten by the stable fly, (*Stomoxyz calcitrans L*).

The intended method of emptying the manure bunkers should be established early on. The most frequently used method is for the work to be subcontracted. Usually the manure is loaded on to a tall-sided trailer by a mechanical crab for removal from site. With this method, the height of the bunker sides will be dictated by the vision position of the driver operating the crab, the optimum maximum height of the wall being 2.2 m (7 ft).

The design of the manure bunker will also be dictated by how the stable hands do the mucking out. In stable

86

Opposite: *Simple entrance in a rural setting.*

Next two pages: *Another simple entrance.*

An ornate entrance to a larger equestrian estate.

yards where the manure is carried out by the stable hand using a rubber basket or skip, the type of manure bunker required may be one constructed half into the ground, thereby reducing the lifting necessary when emptying the manure skip.

Where manure barrows are used the manure bunker is better at ground level, although it is still possible for it to be sunken. In a situation where the mucking out takes place straight on to a tractor/trailer, the bunker must be at ground level to allow complete access for the vehicles. With a ground-level muck bunker there is also the opportunity of using a tipping trailer to build or tip the manure to a higher level, thereby making greater use of the compound. It is important to establish whether a tractor with a spine bucket is to be used to store the manure to greater heights than can be achieved by hand and also the intended frequency of manure removal from site.

One enterprising manager on a recently developed establishment has adopted a very interesting method of manure removal. His method eliminates the necessity for a manure bunker close to each yard and therefore dramatically reduces the problems of vermin, loose straw, flies and smells. It therefore reduces the risk of infection associated with manure bunkers. The system is based on mucking out on to a barrow which is then emptied on to a special walk-on skip strategically placed outside each yard. When full, the skip is transported to a central manure bunker well away from the animals and any living accommodation. This method is convenient for the yard hands and is economical on purchase of equipment, while avoiding the construction cost of several manure bunkers.

Should a conventional manure bunker be necessary, then this should be constructed with impervious walls and floor. Dense blockwork walls are appropriate, with a concrete floor sloping to a drainage point which discharges into a silage tank. It is advisable to arrange the slope of the surrounding area of hard standing away from the manure bunker, otherwise storm water will be directed into the manure bunker, causing the silage tank to fill unnecessarily quickly, again involving excessive emptying costs.

If the manure bunker is to be constructed in brickwork or blockwork, then it is important to have movement joints in the block/brick walls. This is a frequent source of constructional defect and, apart from being untidy in appearance, it can be a hazard should loose bricks/blocks or coping fall.

In the calculation of the size of the manure bunker, as a guide, 0.5 cu m (18 cu ft) of manure should be allowed per box per day if the establishment is using straw. If shavings or shredded paper are used as bedding, then the waste per day is approximately 0.25 cu m (9 cu ft) per day per box.

During storage in the bunker, natural compaction takes place in the order of 10 per cent per week for a 1.8 m (6 ft) high heap. This is in normal weather conditions; in dry periods, the compaction will be less.

With the ever-increasing cost of removal of muck, some establishments are now looking at alternative disposal methods. One method that has been looked at quite closely is incineration. The cost of incineration makes this method uneconomical at the moment but, by recovering the heat for further use, it may well mean that this process will become more common in the future.

Loading ramps

On large and medium sized stable yards there will be the need to locate a loading ramp. This facility will be in frequent use and, from discussion with horse transporter companies, it would seem that many loading ramps are built too narrow and this makes manoeuvring with the transporter very difficult, particularly at night.

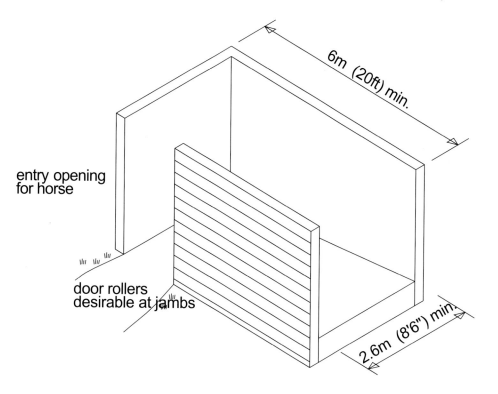

entry opening
for horse

door rollers
desirable at jambs

6m (20ft) min.

2.6m (8'6") min.

Typical loading ramp.

Research into transporter sizes shows that, currently, the majority of loading doors are between 1.8-2.0 m (6-6$\frac{1}{2}$ ft) wide and the length of the loading door is about 2.2 m (7 ft).

The size of a horse transporter can vary from a single-box-type trailer up to a nine-box transporter. The type of establishment will determine the size and location of the loading ramp.

The maximum size of a nine-box transporter is generally 2.4 m wide by 3.6 m high by 13.0 m long (8 x 12 x 43 ft). The height given does not include the aerial but, for peace of mind, the specific dimensions, weights and types of vehicle should be established for each project.

The level of the transporter loading door from the ground is usually between 750 mm and 950 mm (30-37 in) so a loading ramp constructed with a 500 mm (20 in) leading edge will ensure that the horse can be loaded or unloaded on a gentle gradient.

The optimum internal width for the loading ramp should be 2.6 m (8$\frac{1}{2}$ ft) wide, with the length of the loading ramp not less than 5.0 m (16 ft).

The position of the loading ramp should be carefully considered especially if there is the possibility of a foreign transporter vehicle needing to be accommodated as they have the loading doors on the opposite side to British transporters. Enough space should be provided to allow the full length of a lorry to be accommodated.

The site should also be selected so that the area can be covered conveniently by an external light for safe use during darkness.

Whether or not a door is required on the loading ramp, a pair of door rollers is certainly necessary in order to reduce the risk of injury to the animals when being loaded.

Chapter Nine
Maintenance

Nowadays, there is a general tendency to reduce labour costs and one of the first things to be cut is the maintenance budget. In the short term, this has no perceptible effect but rarely is the budget increased to cover past neglect. Ultimately, however, the fabric of the buildings will suffer to the extent that costly remedial action may well be necessary and, in the intervening period, the buildings and estate will take on a neglected look, giving the impression that the establishment is not thriving.

The stable staff should be organised to carry out general maintenance during the slacker periods of the season to avoid the estate becoming neglected.

When the animals are likely to be out in the field all day, this gives the opportunity to steam clean and redecorate the buildings and to carry out general repairs, also to carry out the essential estate management of cleaning out dead wood from hedges and clearing ditches to ensure free-flowing drainage.

A perennial problem with stables is the maintenance that regularly occurs with stable doors swelling, shrinking and sagging. To an extent this is due to wood being a natural product and the effects of sun and rain. The movement and easing of stable doors can be reduced by having them made with a framed construction which, although initially more expensive, is less of a maintenance problem later on. Alternatively, the doors can be specified with a steel frame and hinges and this will virtually eliminate the ongoing maintenance of a carpenter adjusting the doors each season.

Drains should be periodically flushed through and gullies and interceptor cleared of debris. Downpipes and rainwater gutters should be checked for evidence of leakage and any leak tended to immediately as dampness in the structure can quickly lead to longer term damage.

Opposite: *A well-maintained equestrian estate.*

Chapter Ten

Health and safety at work

A recent requirement under the Health and Safety Act concerns the storage of chemicals. A lockable store should now be provided to house chemicals. This should be in a place with good ventilation, and with the ability to be hosed down should a spillage occur. Obviously there also needs to be a drain from the area chosen.

Perhaps one of the best locations for the chemical store is in part of the tack room. Wherever it is situated, however, it must be located for convenient access for use but safe from children.

The storage unit itself should also be secure. Because of the new regulation, several manufacturers have produced purpose self-contained chemical storage cupboards in varying sizes to suit most needs. The units come complete with plumbed in tap ready for connection to a nearby supply.

Opposite: *A fenced in stable yard to stop loose horses escaping.*

Glossary

American barn — stable boxes within a barn enclosure accessible from within the barn

apron — the area immediately outside the stable box

anti-chew strip — a metal strip fixed to timber to stop the horse from chewing it

anti-weave grille — a grille fixed to the top of a stable door, through which a horse can look out

arris — the external angle of an item – usually brickwork or joinery.

auto drinker — a water drinker that automatically fills when the water level drops

building regulations — regulations that control the minimum standard of various buildings

casting rail — a rail fixed to the wall of a box at a level to allow a horse that has rolled on its back to push against the rail in order to get to its feet again

CCTV — closed circuit television

cesspool — an underground tank used to hold effluent

combi-heater — an electric heater that has the facility to store heat at cheap overnight rates, but with an additional convector element for instant heat

Glossary

crib-biting — a tendency to bite and chew any projecting surfaces (usually wooden) available within the stable

crush — a timber or steel apparatus into which the horse is led and secured in order that it can be inspected or attended to in safety

door grille — a grille fitted onto the top of the bottom stable door

door jamb — the side frame of a door opening

door rollers — a circular timber stem fitted on axle brackets to enable the timber to turn freely

fairfaced blockwork — concrete blockwork built neatly, not requiring render or plaster finish

fly mesh — fine mesh used to allow ventilation but which will prevent insects from entering

form — the shape and layout of a building

French drain — a trench filled with shingle incorporating a perforated draining pipe to take away surface water

Green Belt — land defined by statute, which should not be built on unless special circumstances dictate

in situ — constructed or fixed in place

loading ramp — a construction used to enable easy loading of a horse on to a transporter

loose box — a stable box where the horse is untethered

manure bunker — a ground-level walled construction to retain stable waste

muck pit — a partially below-ground excavated construction to retain stable waste

orientation — direction in relation to points of the compass

party wall — a wall dividing two units

planning permission — statutory permission from a local authority required prior to building

plastic cracking — fine surface cracking of concrete due to too rapid drying

purlin — a beam supporting the roof

RCB — residual circuit breaker – a device to cut off electrical power

Section 106 Agreement	a legal agreement restricting planning permission by conditions	*teaser*	a stallion used to test a mare's receptiveness prior to her being taken to be covered by the nominated stallion
septic tank	an underground effluent storage tank that allows liquid waste to pass through	*teasing board*	a timber panel approx. 1.5 m high by 3 m (5 ft x 10 ft) long where mares are tested for oestrogen to see if they are ready to receive the stallion
shelter belt	a hedge or line of trees to provide shelter against the elements		
		thermal mass	dense materials able to equalise fluctuations in temperature
silage tank	a fully enclosed tank set underground to collect effluent	*trace heating*	thin wire elements wrapped around pipes to stop them freezing
soakaway	an underground chamber, either empty or filled with clean hardcore, into which storm water drains discharge	*tractor-way*	the access way in the centre of an American barn
soffite	the underside eaves section of a roof	*trash box*	a gully outlet from a drainage channel
stocks	another name for a crush	*vernacular*	shape and style of building and types of materials used in the locality
storage heater	a heater using cheap night-rate electricity which dissipates its heat next day	*window grille*	a metal grille put against a window to protect it
tack room	a room used to store tack such as saddles, bridles etc.	*Yorkshire boarding*	vertical timber slats with gaps between them

Bibliography

A Barn Well Filled, The Blood-Horse.★

Horse Breeding and Stud Management, Henry Wynmalen, Country Life, 1950

Design and Construction of Stables, Peter C. Smith, J. A. Allen, 1967

Respiratory Diseases, Peter Gray, J.A. Allen, 1994

Thoroughbred Breeding, Mordaunt Milner, J. A. Allen, 1987

PPG 7: The rural economy, HMSO – January 1992

★ *A Barn Well Filled* is a book compiled from articles featuring equestrian buildings that have appeared in the American equestrian magazine *The Blood-Horse* over several years.

Index

Index